I0198872

The
Church Member's Guide

by

John Angell James

Solid Ground Christian Books
PO Box 660132 ~ Vestavia Hills AL 35266

SOLID GROUND CHRISTIAN BOOKS
Po Box 660132, Vestavia Hills AL 35266
205-443-0311
sgcb@charter.net
http://solid-ground-books.com

The Church Member's Guide
John Angell James (1785-1859)

Taken from the 1839 US edition by Gould, Kendall & Lincoln

Published by Solid Ground Christian Books

Classic Reprints Series

First printing of hardcover edition April 2003
First printing of paperback edition June 2004

ISBN: 1-932474-03-X (hardcover)
ISBN: 1-932474-33-1 (paperback)

Manufactured in the United States of America

Preface
to the First American Edition

In presenting the following pages to the notice of the American churches, it is necessary to offer some remarks.

During the few past years, God has graciously poured out his Holy Spirit upon various regions of our country. Zion has broken forth on the right hand and upon the left, and has received a vast accession of converts from those who were once aliens from the commonwealth of Israel. The Church has gazed upon her new-born children with delight, and inquired, "As for these, whence did they come?" They are recruits from the world; they are deserters from the army of the prince of the powers of darkness; they have sworn allegiance to another Sovereign, one Jesus. They have identified themselves with his cause, they are subjects of his kingdom; they have become strangers upon the earth, that they may be citizens of heaven, and they seek that better country.

It has been frequently lamented, that there was no work upon Church Fellowship, which could be put into the hands of church members, and especially of our youthful brethren and sisters, embodying under separate heads those scriptural instructions which he dispersed through the Sacred Volume. I have frequently heard the complaint from ministers, "O that we had a directory for our members, that all our churches and all our brethren might be one in discipline and feeling, as well as in doctrine and practice." And since my engagement in pastoral labors, and more especially when lately called to receive a large number of young and inexperienced persons to the fellowship of the church, I have felt that a Church Member's Guide was a desideratum.

After a careful examination of the various works on this subject, which are in circulation in the English churches, I am persuaded that I can render no greater benefit to the Christian church, than by presenting to its attentive regard, the treatise entitled, "Christian Fellowship, or The Church Member's Guide," by the Rev. J.A. James of Birmingham, England. On a careful perusal of the English edition, I was convinced, that though admirably adapted to the state of the British churches, yet it required a *considerable alteration* to render it extensively useful in our western churches, which have so happily come up from the bondage of National Establishment, passed through the wilderness of persecution, and are planted in this thrice happy land, where government does all for Religion which she asks, wishes, or wants; and that is, - *lets her alone.*

Mr. James has displayed singular ability in his defense of the churches which have dissented from the National Establishment; and it is gratifying to see so able a champion, wielding such powerful weapons, with so fearless a temper, in a cause so good and holy as that of Protestant Nonconformity. But the existing relations of Episcopacy and dissent in England, which fully justify Mr. James in carrying his remarks on Law Establishments throughout the volume, having no place among us, it is desirable, and indeed necessary, that all passages of reference to these subjects should be expunged. I may be exposed to the criticism of a few who would blame me for altering an author's work, adding to or diminishing from it; but I find all the shelter that I need from such censure, in the opening remark of Mr. James' Preface: "The chief value of a book consists in its utility." The *entire* civil and religious liberty which we enjoy in this country, has produced habits and sentiments very dissimilar to those which are the result of a different state of society in our father land.

Bearing this fact in view, I have omitted many expressions, left out whole lines and paragraphs, and in some instances altered words, when satisfied that *"utility"* required such a course.

I have pleasure in the belief, that the excellent author would sanction the task which I have assumed; and that to promote the increased service of his work in the cause of Christ, he would permit its accommodation to a meridian very different from that in which its circulation was primarily designed.

May the Head of the church smile on this effort to advance the purity and happiness of that body which he purchased with his own blood; and may this work serve to render the members of the church a peculiar people, zealous for good works.

J.O. Choules

Newport, Rhode Island, March 30, 1829

Preface to the Stereotype Edition

The high estimation in which The Church Member's Guide is held by the religious public has been evinced in the rapid sale of three editions. The editor, in preparing the first edition, turned his attention chiefly to an omission of all that related to the points of debate between the established church and the English dissenters; but as the demand for the work is become so general in all parts of the country, that the publishers have determined to stereotype it, a very careful revision has been made, and some sentences omitted which may accommodate the volume still farther to the state of American churches. It is gratifying to the editor to receive continued assurances that the Guide is effecting much good. May it elicit the energies of the Church. She has a giant's strength, but it is in repose.

The discipline and order of God's house should not be neglected. Personal piety, social religion, the majesty of truth, and the diffusion of the gospel, are all connected with the constitution and discipline of the churches in the same degree as a cause and effect.

Newport, April 1, 1831

Author's Original Preface

The chief value of a book consists in its utility. We may be surprised by what is original, amused by what is entertaining, and dazzled by what is splendid; but we can be benefited only by what is good. To discover new territories in the world of thought is an effort of genius to which few can aspire. Every sailor cannot be a Columbus; but the labors of the pilot are not to be despised, because they are restricted to the humbler task of conducting the voyager through seas and shoals long known to geography: at any rate, he has fascilitated the pursuits of the established trade, if he has not opened new fields for the exploits of commercial enterprise. Such are the pretensions of the author of the following treatise; he aspires to no loftier character than a guide through channels which, although intricate, are certainly not new.

The author has treated the subject of church government more in a practical than in a controversial manner. Numerous are the votive offerings which already hang around this compartment of the temple of truth; but they are too generally composed of, or attended with, a chaplet of thorns. In this treatise, the author has endeavored to sacrifice, at the same time, to both truth and love, whose altars should ever be near each other. He has endeavored to state his own opinions with clearness and boldness, but, at the same time, without dogmatism or asperity. His aim has been rather to regulate the spiritual police of our Zion, than either professedly to strengthen its bulwarks, or to increase its means of spiritual conquest; assured that it is most mighty, when it is most holy and peaceful; and that love and purity render our churches "bright as the sun, fair as the moon, and terrible as an army with banners."

As the form of church government here exhibited, so far as human direction is concerned, allows of a considerable share of popular influence, the author has adopted two general principles, to which he has given great prominence in the following pages; and these are, the absolute impropriety of a few rich men attempting to lord it over God's heritage, and the equal impropriety on the part of those who are young, or immature in knowledge and experience, practically asserting their claim to equal rights, upon every occasion, in a vehement and contentious manner. In all societies, there necessarily must be some individuals of greater influence than the rest; but this influence should ever be the result of character and usefulness, rather than of station; and should be most cheerfully conceded by others, but never forcibly taken by themselves.

If the author has been acquainted with any treatise on this subject, in which the principles here laid down and illustrated, had been sufficiently developed, he would have spared himself the trouble of this production. The little tract of Dr. John Owen's, entitled "Eschol," the addresses of Dr. Harris and Mr. Hacket, and the Catechism of Mr. Miller, are exceedingly excellent; and the only fault belonging to them, which the author has any hope of correcting in his book, is their brevity. The compendium of the late Rev. Daniel Turner, of Abingdon, is very useful as a skeleton; but a mere unclothed synopsis of principles, unaccompanied by much illustration, is not sufficiently attractive for ordinary readers, who need not only to be informed what is their duty, but allured to its performance. Mr. Inne's "Sketches of Human Nature" are judicious to admiration, and have furnished many valuable remarks to enrich the following work; but do not so directly and comprehensively treat on the subject of church government, as to render this volume unnecessary.

As the author not only renounces all claims to infallibility, but is sorrowfully conscious of liability to error; and as he is anxious to render this little work as useful as possible, he will be most happy, in case of its coming to a second edition, to avail himself of the hints of his brethren, and the remarks of *friendly* critics, in order to render it more worthy of public esteem, and more adapted to general usefulness. It is more than probable that on such a subject his views will be opposed by some; and the moment they are shown to be opposed to the Scripture, he will abandon them himself, and thank the man who has convinced him of his error.

Edgbaston, June 15, 1822

CONTENTS

CHURCH MEMBER'S GUIDE.

CHAPTER I.

ON THE NATURE OF A CHRISTIAN CHURCH.

IT is obviously incumbent on the members of any community, whether civil or sacred, to acquaint themselves with its constitution and design ; without this, they can neither adequately enjoy the privileges, nor properly discharge the duties, which their membership brings with it. Such persons are held more by feeling than by principle ; a tenure quite insufficient, as a bond of religious connexion.

It is admitted that as in the human frame, so in the system of divine truth, there are parts of greater and less importance : and the man who would put the principles of church government upon a level with the doctrine of the atonement, and represent a belief in the former as no less essential to salvation than a reliance upon the latter, betrays a lamentable ignorance of both. Still, however, although the hand is of less consequence to vitality than the head or the heart, is it of no value ? Will any one be reckless of his members, because he can lose them and yet live ? So because church government is of less moment to spiritual and eternal life than faith in Christ, will any one abandon it as a vain and profitless su'ject ? Whatever God has made the subject of revealed truth, should be guarded, on that account, from being considered as too frivolous to deserve our attention.

The government of the church ought never to be viewed apart from its moral and spiritual improvement, any more than the laws of a country should be considered as something distinct from the means of its civil order, comfort, and strength. It is impossible for us to imagine otherwise, than that the Head of the church arranged its government with a direct reference to its purity and peace, and that the system he has laid down is the best calculated to promote these ends. Hence, then, it is obviously our duty to inquire what that system is, not merely for its own sake, but for the sake of the interests of evangelical piety. The error of viewing the subject of church government as a mere abstract question, is very common, and has tended more than any thing else, with many persons, to lead them to regard it with indifference and neglect. The acknowledgment of no other rule of faith and practice than the word of God, must tend to exalt the only infallible standard of truth, and the only divine means of sanctity—the refusal to own any other head of the church than Christ, must bring the soul into more direct submission to him—the scheme of founding a right to spiritual privileges exclusively on the scriptural marks of religious character, and not upon legislative enactments, or national dissent, must have a tendency to produce examination, and prevent delusion—and indeed the habit of viewing the whole business of religion as a matter of conscience, and not of custom, to be settled between God and a man's own soul, must ensure for it a degree of attention more solemn and more effectual than can be expected, if it be allowed, in any degree, to rank with the affairs which are regulated by civil legislation.

It will probably be contended by some, in apology for their neglect, that the New Testament has laid down no specific form of church government, and that where we are left without a guide, it is useless to inquire if we are following his directions. If by this it be meant to say, that the Lord Jesus Christ has left us no apostolic precept or example, which is either directory for our practice, or obligatory upon our conscience, in the formation of Christian societies, nothing can be more erroneous. It might be presumed, *a priori*, that a matter of such moment would not be left so unsettled, and we have only to look into the Word of God, to see how groundless is the assertion. It is true that we shall search the New Testament in vain for either precedent or practice, which will support *all* the usages of our churches, any otherwise than as these usages are deduced from the spirit and bearing of general principles. These alone are laid down by the apostles, but still with sufficient precision to enable us to determine whether the Episcopal, the Presbyterian, or Independent form of church government, be most consonant with the mind and will of Christ.

What is a Christian church?

The word *church* signifies an assembly. In the New Testament it invariably applies to persons, not to places. It means not the building in which the assembly is convened, but the assembly itself. It has an enlarged, and also a more confined signification in the Word of God. In some places it is employed to comprehend the aggregate of believers of every age and nation; hence we read of the " general assembly and church of the first born," and of the church which " Christ loved and purchased with his blood." Acts xx. 28. In its more confined acceptation, it means a congregation of professing Christians, meeting for worship in one place ; hence we read of the church at Corinth, of the Thessalonians, of Ephesus, &c.   These are the only two senses in which the word is ever employed by the sacred writers ; consequently all provincial and national churches, or, in other words, to call the people of a province or nation a church of Christ, is a most gross perversion of the term, and rendering the kingdom of Jesus more a matter of geography than of religion.   The sacred writers, when speaking of the Christians of a whole province, never employ the term in the singular number ; but, with great precision of language, speak of the *churches* of Galatia, Syria, Macedonia, Asia, &c.

A church of Christ, then, in the latter and more usual acceptation of the term, means " a number of professing Christians, united to each other by their own voluntary consent, having their proper officers, meeting in one place for the observance of religious ordinances, and who are independent of all other control than the authority of Christ expressed in his word."   This company of professing Christians may be few or many in number, rich or poor in their circumstances, and may meet either in a mean or magnificent building, or in no building at all.   These things are purely adventitious ; for, provided they answer to the above definition, they are still, to all intent and purpose, a church of Christ.

I.   *The members of the church should be such as make a credible profession of their faith in Christ ;* or, in other words, such as appear to be regenerated by the Spirit of God, to have believed in the Lord Jesus for salvation, and to have submitted themselves in their conduct to the authority of his word. To these the Head of the church has limited the privileges of his kingdom ; they alone can enjoy its blessings, and perform its duties; and to such the Epistles are uniformly addressed, Romans i. 7. 1 Cor. i. 2. &c. If these passages are read, it will be found that the members of the first churches are not merely admonished *to be* saints, but are addressed *as such;* which is a circumstance of great weight in determining the question about the proper subjects of fellowship. But who is to judge in this case? I answer, the church; for although no instance can be brought from the New Testament, in which any one of the primitive churches can be proved to have exercised this power, yet, as it is a voluntary society, founded on the principle of mutual affection, it seems reasonable that the church should judge of the existence of those qualifications which are necessary to the enjoyment of communion. The very act of obtruding upon them any one without their own consent, whether by a minister or by elders, is destructive of one purpose of Christian association,—i. e. the fellowship of the brethren. Nor is the power of searching the heart requisite for those who exercise the right of admitting others, since we are to judge of each other by outward conduct.

II. This company of professing Christians *must meet in one place for the observance of religious institutes.* A society that cannot associate, an assembly that cannot assemble, are perfect solecisms. When, therefore, a church becomes too large to communicate at one table, and divides, to eat the Lord's supper, in two distinct places of worship, each having its own pastor, there are two churches, and no longer one only.

III. These persons must be formed into a society upon the principle of *mutual voluntary consent.* They are not to be associated by act of civil govern-

ment, by ecclesiastical decree, by ministerial authority, or by any other power than that of their own
unconstrained choice.   They are to give themselves
first to the Lord, and then to each other.   No
authority whatever, of an earthly nature, is to con-
strain them to unite themselves in fellowship, nor
to select for them any particular company of believers
with whom they shall associate.   All is to be the
result of their own selection.   Parochial limits,
ecclesiastical divisions of country, together with all
the commands of ministerial authority, have nothing
to do in regulating the fellowship of the saints.
The civil power, when employed to direct the affairs
of the church of Christ, is manifestly out of place.
It is as much at a man's own option, so far as human
authority is concerned, to say with whom he will
associate in matters of religion, as it is to decide
who shall be his fellows in philosophical or literary
pursuits.

IV.   A church of Christ has its *scriptural officers*.
Here two questions arise :—First, How many kinds
of officers does the New Testament mention?
Secondly, How are they to be chosen?   As to the
kinds of office-bearers in the primitive churches,
there can be neither doubt nor difficulty with any
one who will impartially consult the Word of God.
With all that simplicity which characterizes the
works of God, which neither disfigures his produc-
tions with what is excrescent, nor incumbers them
with what is unnecessary, he has instituted but two
kinds of permanent officers in his church, bishops
and deacons; the former to attend to its spiritual
affairs, and the latter to direct its temporal concerns.
That there were but two, is evident, because we
have no information concerning the choice, qualifications, or duties of any other.   The bishops of the

primitive churches correspond exactly to the pastors of modern ones. That bishop, elder, and pastor, are only different terms for the same office, is evident from Acts xx. 17, compared with the 28; Titus i. 5, 7, and 1st Peter v. 1, 2. They are called bishops, which signifies overseers, because they overlook the spiritual concerns, and watch for the souls of their brethren, Acts xx. 28, 1st Tim. iii. 1. Pastors or shepherds, because they feed the flock of God with truth, Ephes. iv. 11. Rulers, because they guide the church, Heb. xiii. 7. Elders, because of their age, or of their possessing those qualities which age supposes, Tit. i. 5. Ministers, because they are the servants of Christ and the gospel. Ephes. vi. 21.

The *Deacon* is appointed to receive and distribute the funds of the church, especially those which are raised for the relief of the poor. All other kinds of officers than these two, are the inventions of men, and not the appointment of Christ; and which, by intending to add splendour to the kingdom of Jesus, have corrupted its simplicity, destroyed its spirituality, and caused it to symbolize with the kingdoms of this world.

On the mode of electing them to their office the Scripture is sufficiently explicit, to justify the practice of those denominations who appeal to the suffrages of the people. If the Acts of the Apostles be studied with care, a book which seems given us more for the regulation of ecclesiastical practices, than the revelation of theological opinions, we shall find that nothing was done in the primitive churches without the cooperation of the members; *no, not even when the apostles themselves were present.* Even the election of a new apostle was made by the brethren, and not by the ministers exclusively. Acts

i. 21, 26. The deacons were chosen by the same persons. Acts vi. The decrees of the council at Jerusalem were passed also by them, and went forth with their name. Acts xv. 23. From hence we infer, that although no case occurs in the inspired history, where it is mentioned that a church elected its pastor, yet it so entirely accords with the practice of the church in other respects, that an exception in this particular would have been a singular anomaly, which nothing could justify but the plainest and most express provision. The decisions of *reason* harmonize, on this subject, with the testimony of revelation; for if we have an undoubted right to choose our own lawyer, or physician, how much more so, to elect the man to whom we shall intrust the care of our soul! If we should feel it hard to be obliged to take the medicines of the parish doctor, whether we liked them or not, how much more oppressive is it, that we should be obliged to hear the opinions of the parish minister, who may have been appointed by the patron for other qualifications than those of a spiritual nature, and whose sentiments may be as much opposed to the doctrines of the gospel, as his conduct is to its holiness! What! are we to be obliged to look up to such a man as our spiritual instructer, because some profligate, who has the living in his gift, chooses to introduce him to the vacant pulpit?

V. A Christian church, with its office-bearers, is *complete within itself,* for the observance of divine ordinances, and the exercise of discipline; and is subject to no authority or tribunal on earth. This is the Congregational or Independent form of church government, and it is thus denominated, to distinguish it from the Episcopal, or the government of a bishop, and from the Presbyterian, or the government of the churches by the authority of their assembled pastors and elders. No trace of any foreign control over a church of Christ, can be found in the New Testament, except such as the representatives of Jesus Christ.

VI. Such a church *is bound, by the authority of Christ, in their associated capacity,* to observe all the institutes, to obey all the commands, and to cherish all the dispositions, which relate to their social union, in the time, order, and manner in which they are enjoined by Christ Jesus. They are to assemble in public on the first day of the week for prayer, praise, hearing the Scriptures read and expounded, celebrating the Lord's supper, and exercising mutual affection. They are also bound by divine authority to maintain the purity of the church, by receiving only such as give evidence of true faith, and by excluding from their communion all those whose life is opposed to the doctrine which is according to godliness. They are to live in the exercise of mutual submission and brotherly love, and ever to consider themselves amenable to the tribunal of Christ, for their conduct in their church capacity.

Such is a very concise view of the nature of a Christian church.

Hence what might be termed the *general* principles of the New Testament on this topic, are the all-sufficiency and exclusive authority of the Scriptures as a rule of faith and practice in matters of religion ;—the consequent denial of the right of legislatures and eccelesiastical conventions to impose any rites, ceremonies, observances, or interpretations of the Word of God, upon our belief and practice ;—the unlimited and inalienable right of every man to expound the Word of God for himself, and to worship his Maker in that place and

2

manner which he deems to be most accordant with
the directions of the Bible ;—the utter impropriety
of any alliance or incorporation of the church of
Christ with the governments of the kingdoms of
this world ;—the duty of every Christian to oppose
the authority which would attempt to fetter his conscience with obligations to religious observances
not enjoined by Christ. These are general principles, which should lead the thinking Christian to
separate from all national establishments of religion
whatever.

It is not enough to plead the authority of example, or of mere feeling, as a reason for any religious
service. These are insufficient pilots on the troubled ocean of theological opinion, where opposing
currents, stormy winds, and concealed rocks, endan-
ger the safety of the voyager to eternity. Our compass is the word of God, reason must be the steers-
man at the helm to guide the vessel by the direction
of the needle, and that mariner is accountable for the
consequences, who is too ignorant or too indolent
to examine his course.

Away with that morbid insensibility which exclaims, " It is of no consequence to what church or
denomination a man belongs, provided he be a
Christian." Such a spirit is a conspiracy against
the throne of truth, and is the first step towards a
complete abandonment of the importance of right
sentiments. Admitting that error is to be measured
by a graduated scale, who will undertake to fix upon
the point where harmless mistakes end and mischievous ones begin ? Every thing relating to religion is
of consequence. In the temple of truth, not only the
foundation is to be valued and defended, but every
point and every pinnacle.

It does not necessarily follow that an inquiry

into the grounds of our conduct should imbitter our temper. The mist of passion obscures the splendour of truth, as much as fogs do the effulgence of the solar orb. Let us contend earnestly for right principles, but let it be in the exercise of right feelings. Let us hold the truth in love. Then do our sentiments appear to greatest advantage, and look like gems set in gold, when they are supported by a spirit of Christian charity.

"O divine love! the sweet harmony of souls! the music of angels! the joy of God's own heart; the very darling of his bosom! the source of true happiness! the pure quintessence of heaven! that which reconciles the jarring principles of the world, and makes them all chime together! that which melts men's hearts into one another! See how St. Paul describes it, and it cannot choose but enamour your affections towards it;—" Love envieth not, it is not puffed up, it doth not behave itself unseemly, seeketh not her own, is not easily provoked, thinketh no evil, rejoiceth not in iniquity; beareth all things, believeth all things, hopeth all things, endureth all things." I may add, it is the best natured thing, the best complexioned thing in the world. Let us express this sweet harmonious affection in these jarring times; that so, if it be possible, we may tune the world into better music. Especially in matters of religion, let us strive with all meekness to instruct and convince one another. Let us endeavour to promote the gospel of peace, the dove-like gospel, with a dove-like spirit. This was the way by which the gospel at first was propagated in the world. "Christ did not cry nor lift up his voice in the streets; a bruised reed he did not break, and the smoking flax he did not quench; and yet he brought forth judgment unto victory." He whispered the

gospel to us from mount Sion, in a still voice ; and
yet the sound thereof went out quickly throughout all
the earth.   The gospel at first came down upon
the world gently and softly, like the dew on Gid-
eon's fleece ; and yet it quickly penetrated through
it ; and, doubtless, this is still the most effectual way
to promote it farther.   Sweetness and ingenuity
will more command men's minds, than passion,
sourness, and severity ; as the soft pillow sooner
breaks the flint than the hardest marble.   Let us
" follow truth in love ;" and of the two, indeed, be
contented rather to miss of the conveying a specu-
lative truth, than to part with love.   When we
would convince men of any error by the strength
of truth, let us withal pour the sweet balm of love
upon their heads.   Truth and love are two of the
most powerful things in the world ; and when they
both go together, they cannot easily be withstood.
The golden beams of truth, and the silken cords of
love, twisted together, will draw men on with a
sweet violence, whether they will or no.

  " Let us take heed we do not sometimes call
that zeal for God and his gospel, which is nothing
else but our own tempestuous and stormy passion.
True zeal is a sweet, heavenly, and gentle flame,
which maketh us active for God, but always within
the sphere of love.   It never calls for fire from
heaven to consume those that differ a little from us
in their apprehensions.   It is like that kind of lightning, (which the philosophers speak of,) that melts
the sword within, but singeth not the scabbard : it
strives to save the soul, but hurteth not the body.
True zeal is a loving thing, and makes us always
active to edification, and not to destruction.   If we
keep the fire of zeal within the chimney, in its own
proper place, it never doth any hurt ; it only warm-

eth, quickeneth, and enliveneth us; but if once we let it break out, and catch hold of the thatch of our flesh, and kindle our corrupt nature, and set the house of our body on fire, it is no longer zeal, it is no heavenly fire, it is a most destructive and devouring thing. True zeal is an *ignis lambens*, a soft and gentle flame, that will not scorch one's hand; it is no predatory or voracious thing; but carnal and fleshly zeal is like the spirit of gunpowder set on fire, that tears and blows up all that stands before it. True zeal is like the vital heat in us, that we live upon, which we never feel to be angry or troublesome; but though it gently feed upon the radical oil within us, that sweet balsam of our natural moisture, yet it lives lovingly with it, and maintains that by which it is fed: but that other furious and distempered zeal, is nothing else but a fever in the soul.

To conclude, we may learn what kind of zeal it is, that we should make use of in promoting the gospel, by an emblem of God's own, given us in the Scripture, those fiery tongues, that upon the day of Pentecost sat upon the Apostles: which sure were harmless flames, for we cannot read that they did any hurt, or that they did so much as singe an hair of their heads."*

---

* Cudworth's Sermon before the House of Commons, 1647.

CHAPTER II.

ON THE NATURE AND DESIGN OF CHURCH FELLOWSHIP.

"For want of clear information on this head, there is, both before and after admission, in the minds of many persons, a certain mystic obscurity hanging over the subject, which either repels them from seeking for admission, or fills them with disquiet. Christian churches have no mysteries, no *adyta*, no secrets. It is a pernicious policy which would exalt plain duties into secret rites, and transform the simple institutions of the gospel into enigmas."* Nothing is more plain than the nature of Christian fellowship, yet nothing is less understood.

I. Church fellowship is *the exercise of the social principle in matters of religion, and in obedience to the authority of Christ.*

Many persons seem to imagine that the only end and object of church fellowship, is the participation of the Lord's supper. Hence they attach no other idea to a church, than that of a company of Christians going together to the sacramental table ; who having nothing to do with each other, till they arrive there, and whose reciprocal duties end with that ordinance. The observance of the Lord's supper, it is confessed, is one design and exercise of fellowship ; but it is not the only one. Man is a social being, by which we mean that he instinctively seeks the company of his fellows ; is capable of enjoying their society, and derives from their communion no small portion of his improvement and felicity

---

* Eclectic Review, vol. 18, p. 325.

The aphorism of Solomon is as just as it is beautiful,—" As iron sharpeneth iron, so a man sharpeneth the countenance of his friend." *Social* bliss was the finish of paradisiacal happiness; its influence has survived the shock of our apostasy, and will be felt amidst the felicities of the heavenly state. It is not matter of surprise, therefore, that the Lord Jesus should recognize the social principle in the arrangements of his wise and merciful economy. He might have left his people unconnected by any visible bond, or at best with no other guide to each other than the natural workings and affinities of the human bosom. Instead of this, however, he has by explicit authority grafted the duties of his religion upon the propensities of our social nature. The identifying law of Christ's kingdom is love to one another; and in order that this love may be more perfect in its exercise, we are united in visible communion. When, therefore, we join a Christian church, we enter a society of believers for the purpose of giving and receiving every suitable expression of mutual love. We then associate ourselves with those towards whom we are to cherish, in consequence of a common relationship, the kindest emotions. We are not only to worship with them in the same place, not only to sit with them at the same sacramental board, but we are to consider ourselves as one of their fellowship, to identify our best feelings with theirs, and in all things to consider ourselves members one of another. Our fellowship is not intended for, nor is it to be expressed by, any one exclusive act; but it is to extend itself to every possible way of having communion with each other. We are to rejoice together in the common salvation; and to bring forth together the fruits of a like precious faith. Dr. Watts has

very beautifully expressed the feelings which every
church member, who understands his relationship,
constantly recognizes.

> " My soul shall pray for Zion still,
> Whine life or breath remains ;
> There my best friends, my kindred dwell ;
> There God my Saviour reigns."

The great end of Christian fellowship, and the
impropriety of limiting its design to a celebration
of the eucharist, are strikingly represented by Mr.
Hall ;—" Nothing is more certain than that the
communion of saints is by no means confined to
one particular occasion, or limited to one transac-
tion, such as that of assembling around the Lord's
table ; it extends to all the modes by which believers recognize each other as the members of a common Head.   Every expression of fraternal regard,
every participation in the enjoyments of social worship, every instance of the unity of the Spirit exerted
in prayer and supplication, or in acts of Christian
sympathy and friendship, as truly belong to the
communion of saints, as the celebration of the eucharist.   In truth, if we are strangers to communion with our fellow Christians on other occasions,
it is impossible for us to enjoy it there ; for the
mind is not a piece of mechanism which can be set
a going at pleasure, whose movements are obedient
to the call of time and place.   Nothing short of an
habitual sympathy of spirit, springing from the cul-
tivation of benevolent feeling, and the interchange
of kind offices, will secure that reciprocal delight,
that social pleasure, which is the soul of Christian
communion.   Its richest fruits are frequently reserved for private conference, like that in which the two
disciples were engaged, in their way to Emmaus,

when their hearts burned within them, while the Lord opened to them the Scriptures. When they take sweet counsel together as they go to the house of God in company, when they bear each other's burdens, weep with those that weep, and rejoice with them that rejoice ; say, have Christians no mutual fellowship ?

The sacred historian has given us a very beautiful practical exhibition of the ends of Christian fellowship in Acts ii. 40—47 : " Then they that gladly received his word were baptized : and the same day there were added unto them about three thousand souls. And they continued steadfastly in the apostles' doctrine and fellowship, and in breaking of bread, and in prayers. And fear came upon every soul : and many wonders and signs were done by the apostles. And all that believed were together, and had all things common ; and sold their possessions and goods, and parted them to all *men*, as every man had need. And they, continuing daily with one accord in the temple, and breaking bread from house to house, did eat their meat with gladness and singleness of heart, praising God, and having favour with all the people. And the Lord added to the church daily such as should be saved."

Here we see the social principle putting forth all its energies in a way of sacred fellowship, and with direct reference to religion. A new and holy brotherhood was set up, of which love to Christ, and to each other for Christ's sake, was the bond. There was the recognition of a common relationship, and the exercise of all that affection which it involved. The converts immediately gave themselves to each other, as members one of another, and not only performed acts of religious worship together, but exercised a reciprocal and most sub-

3

stantial benevolence, and afforded the most valuable
mutual service.

"Imagination can scarcely delineate a scene more
amiably interesting, than that which the infant
church in reality displayed. Bound together by
the fellowship of sentiments, feeling, and affection—having one Lord, one faith, one baptism—the
believers in Christ found more than a compensation
for the contempt, and hatred, and persecution of
the world, in their common hopes, and mutual offices
of kindness. Around them was a scene of rude
agitation and wild confusion; but within the little
circle of their society all was union, harmony, and
love." Alas, alas, that this reign of love and peace
should be of such short duration, that the apostles
lived to witness, not indeed its termination, but its
interruption, and had to interpose their authority to
stop the progress of false opinions, and the alienation of heart to which error had given rise.

This exercise of the social principle is conducted
with direct reference to the authority of Christ.
He who is our Lord has *commanded* it. It is his
will that his people should not live solitarily and
unconnected, but in visible association. To the
question, therefore, Why are you a church member?—the first answer must be, Because Jesus
Christ has commanded it. Independently of the advantages arising from this practice, the true ground
of it is the authority of our divine Lord. It is not
only a privilege which he has permitted us to enjoy,
but a duty which he has commanded us to perform.
If we were unable to perceive its advantages, it
would still be our duty to comply with it. Church
fellowship is no less a duty than the observance of
the first day Sabbath, as the same reasons may be
advanced for one as for the other.

From not viewing it in this light it is, that so many refuse to join themselves to the church: they consider membership merely in the light of a privilege which it is at their option to receive or refuse. This is a very great and very injurious error. If a believer remain without visible connexion with some Christian society, he is guilty of direct disobedience against his rightful Lord.

II. Fellowship *is the instituted way of making a public profession of the faith and hope of the gospel.*

A man may hold the opinions and approve the practices of some voluntary, worldly society; but until he has united himself with it, he is not considered, either by its members or the public, as one of their number. His actually joining himself to them according to the established usage, is his profession. Thus a man may be a sincere believer of the gospel, and, so far as respects his own private conduct, an exemplary example of genuine piety; but until he has connected himself with a Christian church, he has not *professed* himself to be a Christian. It is by that act he declares to the world his faith and hope as a believer in Christ. It is thus he virtually says, "I receive the opinions, possess the dispositions, submit to the obligations, and observe the practices of the church of God with which I now connect myself." Jesus Christ has made it our duty not only to receive his truth into our hearts, but to confess him before men; and it is a duty on which very considerable stress is laid. This is to be done, not in any ostentatious way, but by joining ourselves to his people: which is a confession, that both the church and the world clearly understand. Hence it is apparent, that church membership is no trifling matter, since it is calling heaven, earth, and hell, to witness our solemn declaration of submission to the authority of Christ. It is saying, in the hearing of more worlds than one, "I am a Christian."

III. It is *the visible bond of union with the disciples of Jesus.*

Christians are not only to be united, but are to *exhibit* their union. Their oneness of sentiment, of affection, of purpose, is to be seen. We are not only to love one another, but our love is to be known, which is impossible without membership. In its collective capacity, a church concentrates, as in a focus, the light and love that exist in her individual members. Without being combined in a *visible* union, its splendour would be only as the dim and scattered light which was diffused over the chaos in the twilight of creation, while the fellowship of the saints is the same light gathered up and embodied in the solar orb. We are indeed united in spirit with the church of Christ, from the moment we have believed his gospel; but our union is neither expressed nor recognized, until we have joined it in the usual way. We are citizens in feeling and intention, but not yet known from enemies, aliens, and spies. Membership, therefore, is the bond of visible union with the brethren in Christ.

IV. It is *an explicit declaration of our determination to submit to the government and discipline of the church.*

Every society has laws for the regulation of its affairs. Without these it could not exist; and to which every member professes, at the time of his entrance, his determination to submit. The church of the Redeemer has in like manner its social rules, which respect the members in their associated capacity. We are therefore not only amenable to the direct authority of Christ, but also to that authority express-

ed by the voice of the church; we must submit to
all its regulations, observe all its injunctions, support its decisions, or we can no longer remain
in its communion. If we are called before it, we
must appear; if required to explain any part of our
conduct, we must comply; if censured, we must
submit. We are in no case haughtily to exclaim, "What is the church, that I should obey it?
to my own master I stand or fall." Our act of joining the society is an explicit declaration of our willingness to submit to the laws by which it is governed. We can voluntarily secede when there is
just occasion, or in case of a false decision, we can
mildly protest; but as long as we continue members
we must submit, for our very membership professes
and requires it.

V. It is designed *to exhibit upon a smaller scale
that sublime and glorious union and communion
which subsist, not only between all real Christians of
every country, name, and age, but between the whole
redeemed church and their Divine Head.*

Passages of a very striking import speak of this
most comprehensive confederation. "That in the
dispensation of the fulness of times, he might gather together in one all things in Christ, both which
are in heaven and which are on earth; even in
him." Ephes. i. 10. "There is one body and one
spirit." Ephes. iv. 4. "That which we have seen
and heard, declare we unto you, that ye also may
have fellowship with us; and truly our fellowship
is with the Father and with his Son Jesus Christ."
1 John i. 3. From these passages we learn that
the aggregate of believers, united to Jesus Christ,
and through him to the Father, form one vast harmonious fellowship of holiness and benevolence.
They are united in the same pursuit, which is the

divine glory ; in the same means for the attainment
of that object, which is the salvation of the soul.
The church universal will ever remain the one
grand monument on which are recorded the praises of the living God. Of this general assembly
every particular society is the miniature resemblance. By its public worship, its beautiful subordi-
nation, its mutual affection, its truth, its holiness, its
peace, it is an exhibition to the world of that fellowship which has God in Christ for its head, all believers for its members, heaven for its temple, and
eternity for its duration ; while every time it assem-
bles for worship, it shows forth the unity of the
church, and the communion of saints.

CHAPTER III.

THE PRIVILEGES OF MEMBERSHIP.

" THE privileges of membership are, in a general
sense, the privileges of Christian society : and
churches were originally formed only to secure and
promote these social objects—to bring Christians,
as such, more closely together, to make them known
to each other in that character, and to bind them by
positive engagements to neighbourly offices, religious
communion, and brotherly kindness ;" but to descend
to particulars, these privileges consist in,

I. *The participation of the Lord's supper.*

That a reception of the appointed memorials of
the Saviour's dying love, is indeed a privilege, requires no proof. As creatures, whose minds are
instructed, and whose hearts are impressed through
the medium of our senses, how affecting are the

emblems of the body and blood of Christ! Enough
of resemblance may be observed by the fancy,
between the sign and the thing signified, to aid
the exercise of the affections, while enough of
simplicity remains to prevent the excursions of
the imagination from interfering with the more
sublime and scriptural operations of our faith.
That sacramental seasons are commonly the most
happy and most profitable which a believer ever
spends amongst the means of grace, is a fact not
to be denied. It is no wonder that it should be so.
It is at the sacred supper that the attention is more
powerfully arrested and fixed, and the heart impressed and affected. It is there, that the scheme of redeeming mercy seems peculiarly to expand upon the
understanding, and to excite the emotions of the
bosom in a degree almost unknown elsewhere.
It is there that the glory of the divine character
has been most clearly discovered by our mind; there,
that Jesus has unfolded to us the wonders of his
meditation; and there, that the eternal Spirit has
descended into our souls, in the most munificent
communications of his sanctifying and consoling influence. How have our icy hearts there melted
beneath the ardour of celestial love, and flowed
down in streams of godly sorrow! How have our
grovelling, earthly minds soared, on the wings of
faith and hope, till we have lost sight of earthly
scenes and sounds, amidst the glory of such as are
divine. It is there, that we have felt ourselves
crucified with Christ, and have risen with him into
newness of life. It is there, that brotherly love has
glowed with its most perfect fervour, and the communion of saints has yielded its most precious de-
lights. Happier hours than those which have been
there spent, we never expect to know in this world.

They have left a relish and a fragrance upon the mind; the remembrance of them is sweet, and the anticipation of their return is among the brightest hopes we have this side the vail.

II. Another privilege connected with membership is, *the right of assisting in the choice of a pastor, in the election of deacons, and in the admission and exclusion of members.*

It might indeed be said, that in many cases this right is enjoyed by those who are not church members—be it so; but as it is in *every case* enjoyed by those who *are* members, it may be very fairly placed in the number of their privileges. That it is also in a measure enjoyed by all persons who, in a town where there are more places of worship than one, choose the minister whose preaching they will attend, is also granted; but still there is a great difference between choosing a minister to occupy a particular station, and merely going to hear him when chosen by others.

It must surely be accounted no inconsiderable privilege to have a voice in the election of an individual, on whose ministrations so much of our own spiritual welfare, and that of our families, depends; nor is it a light thing to be admitted to a participation of the other business connected with, and arising from, the history of a church.

III. A church member has the advantage of *pastoral oversight and supplication.*

"They watch for your souls," said the apostle to the ancient Christians, when speaking of their pastors; evidently implying that it was a great privilege to be the subjects of such inspection. A faithful friend, that will instruct, warn, comfort, or reprove, as circumstances may require, is a great treasure; and such an one a Christian will find, or ought to find, in his minister. In him he has a right to expect a steady, active, and vigilant guardian of his eternal interests ; one who will follow the individuals of his charge, as far as can be, through all their spiritual career comforting them when in distress, rousing them when lukewarm, reproving them when their conduct needs rebuke, lending his ear to their every complaint, and opening his heart to receive their every grief. A faithful pastor will consider himself as the guide and the shield of the souls committed to his care ; a shepherd to provide for their wants, a watchman to observe the approach of their dangers. He will visit them in the afflictions which attend their pilgrimage ; will hasten to their bedside when the sorrows of death encompass them ; will disclose to the eye of faith the visions of immortality, which irradiate the dark valley itself ; and will never cease his solicitude until the portals of heaven have closed upon their disembodied spirits.

In addition to this, the pastor bears the church in the arms of his affection, and presents them in his prayers before the throne of grace. Like the high priest of the Jews, he approaches the mercy seat, not with the names of the people merely engraven upon his breast plate, but written upon his heart. Nor does he confine himself to general supplications for the society in the aggregate ; its individual members, in their separate capacity and peculiar circumstances, are often the subjects of his intercession before the fountain of life. As he takes a deep interest in their personal, no less than in their collective capacity, he expresses his concern by definite and special supplication. Not only are sermons composed, but prayers presented, which are adapted to the various cases of his flock. The afflicted, the backsliding, the tempted, the novice, are all in turn remembered in his holiest moments before God. Nor can any of these individuals say to which they are most indebted, to his labours in the pulpit, or to his supplications in the closet; for if "the effectual fervent prayer of the righteous *man* availeth much," we certainly may believe that the entreaty of the righteous *minister* is not less availing.

IV. *The watchfulness, sympathy and prayers of the church*, are no inconsiderable privilege of membership.

In what way these duties should be performed, will be matter of consideration hereafter; and therefore we shall not enter minutely into the subject now, any farther than to show how great a mercy it is to enjoy an interest in the affection and the intercession of a Christian society. We are commanded to exhort one another daily; and amidst such temptations, such weakness, such corruptions as ours, is it not an unspeakable mercy to be surrounded by those who will watch over and assist us? With every help, how hard a thing is it to be a consistent Christian! how difficult to maintain the purity and vigour of true godliness! how often do our steps slip, and our exertions relax! and sometimes, through the deceitfulness of the human heart, others may perceive our danger before we ourselves are aware of its existence. It may often be said of us, as it was of Israel of old, "Strangers have devoured his strength, yet he knoweth it not; grey hairs are here and there upon him, yet he knoweth it not." In such cases, none can estimate the value of those Christian friends, who with faithful love will remind us of our danger, and affectionately admonish us. How inestimable the privilege of having those who will tenderly reprove us, and draw us back with the cords of a man and the bands

of love. In the case of our soul's salvation, more
than worlds are at stake; and he who will give
himself the trouble to admonish us and exhort us
to diligence, performs a service of infinite value,
for which, if we improve by it, we shall offer him
our gratitude in eternity.

And then think of the value of Christian *sympathy*. How consolatory it is in our troubles to
recollect, that there are those who are thinking of
our situation and pitying our distress! Even when
they visit us not, they are probably talking to each
other about us. We have their affectionate remembrance, their tenderest interest.

Nor are their *prayers* withheld when they meet
in the temple, or when they retire to the closet.
When they join with one accord in supplication,
and when they pray to their Father in secret, they
mention their suffering brother or sister, to Him
who loveth the church. Ah! how often has the
troubled believer felt it lighten his load, and irradiate his gloom, as he groaned away the hour when
the church was assembled, to believe that they
were thinking of him, and blessing him with their
prayers! It has been as if an angel were despatch-
ed to inform him that supplication was being made
for him, and that therefore he ought to dry up his
tears. Yes, and the sweet remembrance has in
some cases made the tears forget to fall, and the
half uttered groan to die away with silent submission. He has laid down upon his restless couch
again, and it seemed as if it had been smoothed
afresh for him by some viewless agent; and so it
has, for God has heard the prayers of the church on
his behalf, and has made "all his bed in his sickness."*

* It has been said that the last two particulars are not the
privileges of members exclusively, nor of them as members of a

CHAPTER IV.

THE GENERAL DUTIES OF CHURCH MEMBERS IN THEIR INDIVIDUAL CAPACITY.

I. THEY *should seek to acquire clear and enlarged views of divine truth.*

It is a fact which cannot be questioned, that a very large proportion of those whom we believe to be real Christians are mere babes in knowledge. They have just enough instruction to know that they are sinners, and that salvation is all of grace through Christ Jesus.   But ask them to state, prove,

particular church, but as Christians in general. It is unquestionable, however, that church members have a prior and a stronger claim upon their pastors and each other, for these expressions of sympathy, than any others have ; and it has been admitted, even by those who object to the author's statement, "that churches were originally formed only to secure and promote the social objects of their union—i. e. to bring Christians, as Christians, more closely together, to make them known to each other in that character, and to bind them by positive engagements to neighbourly offices and brotherly kindness ;" if this be correct, as it unquestionably is, then certainly church members, as such, have peculiar claims upon their pastors and each other for neighbourly offices and brotherly kindness ; and who will doubt if this be a privilege ?   One great end of membership, is to found a peculiar claim for these manifestations not merely of Christian, but of brotherly love. If there be no peculiarity of claim above what we have upon each other as Christians, why are we formed into separate churches ?

It appears to me, then, that in addition to the obligation which rests upon me to pray for and watch over my members as Christians, I am bound to take a special interest in their spiritual affairs as members of the church under my care. They stand in a relation totally different from that of persons not in communion, and are entitled far beyond the latter to my sympathy, prayer, and vigilance.

and defend, in a scriptural manner, any one of the leading doctrines of the gospel, and you would immediately discover, how contracted is their view, and how feeble is their perception of divine truth. Instead of walking amidst the splendid light and varied scenery of revelation, with the confidence and joy of men whose vision is clear and strong, they are groping along with the fear and hesitation of those who are partially blind. This, in most cases, is their fault, and not their misfortune merely. We are commanded to grow in knowledge; and the apostle in the following very severe language, reproved the believing Hebrews for their ignorance. " When for the time ye ought to be teachers, ye have need that one teach you again, which be the first principles of the oracles of God." After this he exhorts them to leave the principles of the doctrine of Christ, and go on to perfection. How earnestly, in other parts of his writings, did he supplicate for the churches, an increase of their religious knowledge! Eph. i. 17, 18. Colos. i. 9. It is very common for ministers to complain that they are almost afraid to ascend to the loftier parts of revealed truth, lest a great portion of their hearers, instead of eagerly following them, should reproach them with ascending to barren and almost inaccessible summits.

The *causes* of this deficiency of religious knowledge in our members, are numerous and various. In many cases, the want of a religious education contributes to it. Not a few of them are brought in from the world, when they are far advanced in life. There is, with many, a more culpable cause; I mean a systematic neglect of the subject. " What," they exclaim, " will *head* knowledge do for us? we are for experience ; experience is every thing in religion." What kind of experience that is, which is not founded on knowledge, I am at a loss to conceive. With such people, ignorance appears to be the mother of devotion. It should be recollected that it is in the spiritual world, as it is in the natural; the seed of the kingdom is sown in the light, and light is essential to every stage of its growth. If that be not right knowledge, which does not produce feeling, certainly that is not right feeling which is not produced by knowledge. They who have only head knowledge, dwell in the frigid zone of Christianity; and they who have only feeling, occupy the torrid zone. The former are frozen amidst mere cold and heartless speculation; the latter are scorched amidst wild fanaticism.

How much more real enjoyment of the truth is possessed by him who clearly and comprehensively understands it! and how much more useful is he likely to be in communicating instruction, than the individual who barely understands first principles! Every professing Christian, at least all those who have leisure for reading, should endeavour to unite the knowledge of a good theologian with the experience of a real believer.

In order to this, let Christians set apart time not only for reading, but *studying* the scriptures; let them read theological books which explain and prove the doctrines of the gospel; let them commit to memory the admirable definitions of these doctrines contained in the Assembly's Shorter Catechism; let them attend upon the preaching of the word with a view not only to be comforted, but to be instructed. The exclusive object for which some persons hear sermons, is to obtain a little comfort. They sit waiting and watching for some sweet and savoury assurance, some well known hackneyed consolatory topic, some lively appeal to the experience, and until this comes, they think lightly of every thing else. The minister may have given the clearest elucidation of some dark and doubtful passage, the most profound discussion of some sublime doctrine, the most masterly defence of some disputed truth; but to the mere comfort hunters, all this is nothing else than the husk or the shell, which is to be cracked and thrown away for the kernel of a little Christian experience. From such sermons they go home, with hungry and cheerless appetites, complaining that they have found it a lost opportunity.

Let me not be mistaken. Comfort ought to be sought for, but always through the medium of knowledge. The best warmth is that which comes not from ardent spirits, but from the sun, which sends his heat to the frame, in those beams which convey light to the eye. The fact is, that some people's religion is of that weak, unhealthy kind, which is supported only by elixirs and cordials.

After all, I am constrained to confess, that the darkness which rests upon the mind of the church member, is the result, in some cases, of that cloudiness which envelopes the mind of the pastor; if there is ignorance in the pew, it is because there is so little knowledge in the pulpit. When the preacher dwells on nothing but a few hackneyed commonplace topics of an experimental or consolatory nature; when all the varied and sublime parts of revealed truth are neglected for one unceasing round of beaten subjects; when a text is selected from time to time which requires no study to understand, no ability to expound; when nothing is heard from one Sabbath to another, but the same sentiments in the same words, until the introduction of a new or original conception would startle the congregation almost as much as the entrance of a spectre ; who can wonder, if, under such circumstances, the congregation should grow tired of their preacher ; or if such drowsy tinklings should lull the fold, till with their shepherd they sink to the slumbers of indifference, amidst the thickening gloom of religious ignorance ?

II. *Advancement in religion* is incumbent on every professing Christian.

As the usual mode of admission to our churches, subjects their members to a scrutiny of their conduct, it is considered by many as a kind of ordeal, which being passed with success, remits them from any solicitude about farther improvement. A kind of indelible character is then impressed upon them, which is susceptible of neither increase nor improvement. I do not mean to say that they come deliberately to such a conclusion, or that they are aware of any such opinion being in their mind ; but having passed their trials with honour, they insensibly acquire the idea, that now they are professed and acknowledged Christians, that their religion is admitted to be genuine, that they are put amongst the disciples, and therefore the same anxiety is no longer necessary. Often and often have we seen, especially in the case of young persons, that the act of joining the church, has in some measure diminished the earnestness with which their minds were formerly directed to the subject of religion. They were growing rapidly as babes in Christ, till the consciousness of being a church member, and acknowledged a Christian, either by gencrating pride, or relaxing diligence, has paralyzed their piety, arrested their growth, and left them dwarfs in grace forever after.

We should consider that religion is not an abstract thing of times, places, and ceremonies ; nor is the religious character formed by any single compliance, however public or however solemn. If it were admitted that regeneration is an instantaneous change, in which the whole character of a child of God is formed at once, this will not apply to membership. Instead of considering our union with the church as the goal of our religious career, where improvement may cease, and progress be stopped, we should view it as but the very starting point from whence we are to forget the things that are behind, and press towards the mark for the prize of our high calling. From that moment, we are under more solemn obligations than ever to grow in grace, inasmuch as the means of growth are increased. Till then, we have been as trees growing in obscurity, without the aid of human culture ; but when we associate with a church, we are transplanted into a garden, and have the advantage of the gardener's care, and should therefore abound more than ever in all the fruits of righteousness which are by Jesus Christ unto the glory of God.

III. *Consistency in their conduct,* as professing Christians, is a most obvious and pressing obligation of church members.

The want of this in the conduct of professing Christians has done more harm to Christianity than all the ravings of infidelity from the time of Cain to the death of Paine. This sacred and deathless cause lifts her venerable form, bearing the scars of many a wound, not inflicted by arrows plumed with the pen of Voltaire or Hume ; oh, no, such weapons bounded from her bosom, as from a shield of triple brass, and dropped at her feet to be deposited with the spoils of her victories ; but the darts that lacerated her, and left the memorials of their mischief upon her form, were the vices and follies of her votaries. O Christians ! will *ye* scourge and lacerate

4

her? will *ye* array her in the costume of scorn, and, leading her forth bleeding and dejected to meet her enemies in the gate, proclaim, " Behold, an impostor !"   Will *ye* assist to raise the clamour which infidel philosophers endeavoured to excite, and stir up the multitude to exclaim, " Away with her, away with her!   Crucify her, crucify her !"   Tremble at the thought.   If Christianity ever die, it will not be in the field of conflict, by the power of her enemies, but like Cæsar in the capitol, by the hand of her friends ; and which of us would like to meet the look of her expiring eye, or the mild reproach of her faltering tongue, " What, thou my son !"   But she cannot die ; wounded she may be, and has been ; but the memorials of her injury are the proofs of her immortality, and proclaim her to be of heavenly origin : like the fabled scars of the heathen gods of Greece and Rome, her wounds demonstrably prove that a divinity sustained her.

Still, however, the inconsistencies of professing Christians may limit her reign, although they cannot destroy her existence.   By these things sinners are hardened in their courses, the access to life is rendered more difficult, while the avenues of eternal death are made more wide and easy.   That man, whose conduct opposes his profession, may be certainly arraigned for the crime of murder.   Let him not go quietly to his pillow as if blood-guiltiness were not upon his conscience ; for it *is* there, and a voice is continually saying to him, " Thy brother's blood crieth to me from the ground."   He has not slain the *body* of a fellow mortal, but has been accessory to the death of *souls.*   Some that sought for an apology for their sins, an opiate for their consciences, found it in his misconduct.

I have no need to specify the duties included in

the general idea of consistency; these are known well enough. The apostle's beautiful and comprehensive admonition is a sufficient directory. " Whatsoever things are true, whatsoever things are honest, whatsoever things are just, whatsoever things are pure, whatsoever things are lovely, whatsoever things are of good report, if there be any virtue, and if there be any praise, think on these things."

I particularly exhort church members to beware of what might be denominated the *minor* breaches of consistency. We are not to conclude that nothing breaks the uniformity of our character, but what subjects us to the discipline of the church. Overt acts of immorality are comparatively rare, while ten thousand instances of less delinquency, such as the church cannot take cognizance of, are continually occurring in the conduct of Christians, to the disgrace of religion and the injury of men's souls. Those things are seen in us, which would pass unnoticed in others who make no profession of religion; just as a spot which would be lost on canvass, is visible on cambric. A Christian's character is like polished steel, which may have its lustre destroyed, not only by broad spots of rust, but by an assemblage of innumerable specks.

More scandals have occurred in the Christian church from dishonourable *pecuniary* transactions than from any other source. Instances of drunkenness and debauchery are seldom, compared with those of an artful, imposing, dishonest way of conducting business. The world is a dangerous and successful foe to grace; and although every church member professes himself to be through faith a conqueror, how many by their over-reaching, ungenerous conduct, prove that they are yet enslaved by this sordid enemy. Some there are that betray

their Master for a less sum than that which Judas
set upon his blood; and, for a tithe of thirty pieces
of silver, will be guilty of an action which they
must know, at the time, will provoke the severest
invective and bitterest sarcasm against all religion.

IV. Church members *should excel in the manifestation of the Christian temper.*

The mind which was in Christ Jesus, should be
in them. They should consider *his* character as a
model of their own; and be conspicuous for their
poverty of spirit, meekness, gentleness, and love.
They should seek a large portion of the " wisdom
which cometh from above ; which is first pure, then
peaceable, gentle, easy to be entreated, full of
mercy and good fruits, without partiality and without hypocrisy."   It is matter of surprise and regret,
that many persons seem to think that religion has
nothing to do with the temper; and that provided
they are free from gross sins, and have lively feelings
in devotional exercises, they may be as petulant,
irritable, and implacable as they please.   This is a
dreadful error, and has done great mischief to the
cause of God.   A sour, ill-natured Christian, if I
may describe him by a resemblance as fabulous as
that of the centaur, is like a lamb with a dog's head,
a dove with a vulture's beak, a rose with leaves of
nettles.   If there be any one word which above all
others should describe a Christian's character, it is
that which represents his divine Father; and as it
is said, that God is love, so should it be also affirm-
ed, that a Christian is love—love embodied, an incarnation of love.   His words, conduct, nay, his
very looks, should be so many expressions of love.

V. Church members *should be very eminent for
a right discharge of all their social duties.*

The apostles have given this great importance by the frequency with which they have introduced it.* Christianity, so far from loosening the bands of society, adds to them incredible strength and firmness, by motives drawn from the eternal world. One part of the design of revelation is to purify and strengthen the social principle, and carry it to its greatest elevation and perfection.

A good Christian, and yet a bad husband, father, brother, neighbour, or subject, is an anomaly which the world never yet beheld. Professing Christians should excel all others in the beauties of social virtue. Religion should give additional tenderness to the conjugal relationship; greater love to the parent, and obedience to the child; fresh kindness to the master, and diligence to the servant. The world should look to the church with this conviction, " Well, if social virtue were driven from every other portion of society, it would find an asylum, and be cherished with care, upon the heights of Zion." Then will religion have attained its highest credit upon earth, when it shall be admitted by universal consent, that to say a man is a Christian, is an indisputable testimony to his excellence in all the relations he bears to society.

VI. There are duties to be discharged *in reference to the world.*

By the world, I mean all those of every party and denomination who are destitute of true godliness. The apostle has summed up our obligations towards them under the comprehensive injunction, " Walk in wisdom towards them which are without."† In another place, we are commanded

---

* Ephes. v. 22, vi. 1—9. Col. iii. 18. 1 Tim. vi. 1—4.
1 Pet. iii. 1, 2. 1 Pet. ii. 18.
† Col. iv. 5.

to "Let our light shine before men, that they seeing our good works, may glorify our Father which is in heaven."* We are also exhorted "to have our conversation honest (this word signifies beautiful, honourable) among the Gentiles."† In order to comply with this, we must act consistently with our profession; excel in the observance of social duties; abound in mercy; bear a prudent testimony against evil practices; be most punctiliously exact in fulfilling all our engagements, and performing all our promises; live in a most peaceable and neighbourly manner; perform every office of kindness and charity which can please or benefit; and set an example of industry, honesty, and generosity.

VII. We should as professing Christians *be exemplary in our obedience to the civil magistrate.*

The Scriptures which enjoin this duty are too numerous to be quoted at length.‡ One only shall be given, but that is a very striking one. "Let every soul be subject to the higher powers; for there is no power but of God; the powers that be, are ordained of God. Whosoever therefore resisteth the power, resisteth the ordinance of God: and they that resist shall receive to themselves damnation." This injunction must of course be understood as relating to matters purely civil: or in other words to those laws which are not in opposition to the spirit and letter of divine revelation. If rulers enjoin any thing which is condemned by the word of truth, it is the duty of a Christian, without hesitation, and at all hazards, to act upon the principles, and follow the example of the apostles, and "obey God rather than man."

---

* Matt. v. 16.   † 1 Pet. ii. 12.
‡ Rom. xiii. 1, 2.   Acts xxiii. 5.   Titus iii. 1.   1 Pet. ii. 13, 14.   1 Tim. ii. 1—3.

God forbid I should teach a doctrine so pernicious, as that one of the first efforts of true piety
when it enters the soul is to extinguish the love of
civil liberty; or that having broken the fetters of
vice, it immediately bows the regenerated soul into
submission to the yoke of despotism. No such
thing; religion is a noble, and sublime, and elevat-
ing principle. It expands, not contracts the mind.
It is not a spirit of bondage which causes its pos-
sessor to fear; but it is a spirit of power, and of a
sound mind. It lifts the soul from the dust, and
does not chain it there; it has raised a noble army
of martyrs, every one of whose millions was a hero
that defied the tyrant's rage, and spurned his yoke
Religion therefore is no friend of slavery, nor can
any of its precepts be quoted by the tyrant as an ex
cuse for his trampling on the liberties of mankind.

Avowing thus much, and admitting that the most
spiritual Christian *may* take an interest, and *ought*
to take an interest, in public affairs; nay, that he
ought to maintain a ceaseless jealousy over the
constitution and freedom of his country, still I contend that a constant, and noisy, and factious meddling in party politics, is as injurious to his own
personal religion, as it is to the interest of piety in
general. We do not cease to be citizens, when
we become Christians; but we are in danger of
ceasing to be Christians, when we become politi-
cians. It is with politics as with money; it is not
the temperate use, but the immoderate love of it,
that is the root of all evil. Thousands of professors
of religion have made shipwreck of their faith and
a good conscience, during the tempests of political
agitation; let us then, as we value our lives, be
cautious how we embark on this stormy and troubled ocean.

There is one way in which many Christians offend against the laws of their country without scruple, and without remorse; I mean by endeavouring to evade the payment of taxes. Had there been no Christian statute to condemn this practice, the general principles of reason would be quite sufficient to prove its criminality. But the New Testament has added the authority of revelation to the dictates of reason; and thus made it a sin against God, no less than a crime against society, to defraud the revenue. "Render unto Cesar the things that are Cesar's; tribute to whom tribute is due, and custom to whom custom," is the authoritative language of St. Paul. This precept derives great force from the consideration that it was delivered at a time, and under a government, in which the taxes were not imposed by the people themselves, but by the arbitrary power of a despot. Certainly if, under these circumstances, it was the duty of a Christian to pay the tribute money, any effort which *we* make to evade it, must be additionally criminal, since we are taxed by the will of our representatives. The excuses usually made in justification of this practice, only serve to show how far even some good people may be imposed upon, by the deceitfulness of the human heart. Every time we have made a false return on the schedule which regulates our quota of taxation, or that we have purchased knowingly a contraband article of food, beverage, or dress, we have committed a fraud upon society, have assumed a power to dispense with the laws of our country, have violated the precepts of the New Testament, have brought the guilt of a complicated crime upon our conscience, and have subjected ourselves to the displeasure of God, and the discipline of his church.

CHAPTER V.

ON THE DUTIES OF CHURCH MEMBERS TO THEIR PASTORS.

It is the will and appointment of the Lord Jesus Christ, the King and Head of his churches, that they should behave towards their pastors as his ministers, who come in his name, bear his commands, and transact his business; and who are to be treated, in every respect, in a manner that corresponds with their office. In a subordinate sense, they are ambassadors for Christ, and are to be received and esteemed in a way that corresponds with the authority and glory of the Sovereign who commissions them. Whoever slights, insults, or neglects them, in the discharge of their official duties, disobeys and despises their divine Master, who will keenly resent all the injuries that are offered them. No earthly sovereign will allow his messengers to be rejected and insulted with impunity; much less will the Lord of the church. Those who entertain low thoughts of the pastoral office, and neglect its ministrations; who speak contemptuously of their ministers; who excite a spirit of resistance to their counsels, admonitions, and reproofs; who endeavour to lessen that just reverence, to which, for their works' sake, and on their Master's behalf, they are entitled, certainly despise them, and not only them, but Him that sent them also, and for such conduct will incur the heavy displeasure of Christ, Luke x. 16. 1 Thess. v. 13.

But to descend to particulars; the duty of church members towards their pastors includes:

I. *Submission to their just and scriptural authority.*

5

It is readily admitted that the unscriptural, and therefore usurped domination of the priesthood is the root whence arose the whole system of papal tyranny; which, springing up like a poison tree in the garden of the Lord, withered by its shadow, and blighted by its influence, almost every plant and flower of genuine Christianity. It is matter of no regret, therefore, nor of surprise, if a ceaseless jealousy should be maintained by those who understand the principles of religious liberty, against the encroachments of pastoral authority. Priestly dominion, as it appears in the Vatican, is the most detestable and the most mischievous of all tyranny; but when it appears in the pastor of an independent church, divested at once of the elements of power and the trappings of majesty, the mere mimicry of authority, it is rather ridiculous than alarming, and bears no nearer resemblance to its prototype at Rome, than the little croaking, hopping animal of the pond, did to the ox of the field, which his pride led him to emulate, till he burst.

Still, however, there is authority belonging to the pastor; for office without authority is a solecism. "Remember them that have the rule over you," said St. Paul to the Hebrews, xiii. 7. "Obey them that have the rule over you. Submit yourselves, for they watch for your souls," ver. 17. "They addicted themselves to the ministry; submit yourselves to such." 1 Cor. xvi. 15, 16. These are inspired injunctions, and they enjoin obedience and submission on Christian churches to their pastors. The authority of pastors, however, is not legislative or coercive, but simply declarative and executive. To define with precision its limits, is as difficult as to mark the boundaries of the several colours of the rainbow, or those of light and darkness at the hour of twilight in the hemisphere. This is not the only case, in which the precise limits of authority are left undefined by the Scriptures. The duties of the conjugal union are laid down in the same general manner: the husband is to rule, and the wife to obey; yet it is difficult to declare where, in this instance, authority and submission end. In each of these instances, the union is founded on mutual love, confidence, and esteem, and it might therefore be rationally supposed, that, under these circumstances, general terms are sufficient, and that there would arise no contests for power. If the people see that all the authority of their pastor is employed for their benefit, they will not be inclined to ascertain by measurement whether he has passed its limits. The very circumstance of his prerogative being thus undefined, should, on the one hand, make *him* afraid of *extending* it, and on the other, render his church cautious of *diminishing* it. It is my decided conviction, that, in *some* of our churches, the pastor is depressed far below his just level. He is considered merely in the light of a speaking brother. He has no official distinction or authority. His opinion is received with no deference, his person treated with no respect.

Those persons who are anxious to strip their pastors of all just elevation, cannot expect to derive much edification from their labours; for instruction and advice, like substances falling to the earth, impress the mind with a momentum proportionate to the height from which they descend.

II. Church members should treat their pastor *with distinguishing honour, esteem, and love.*

"Let the elders that rule well be accounted worthy of double honour, especially they that labour in the word and doctrine."* 1 Tim. v. 17. "Knew them that have the rule over you, and esteem them very highly in love, for their works' sake." 1 Thess. v. 11, 12. To prescribe in what way our love should express itself, is almost needless, as love is the most inventive passion of the heart, and will find or make a thousand opportunities for displaying its power. Love is also *practical*, as well as ingenious, and does not confine itself either to the speculations of the judgment, or the feelings of the heart. It breathes in kind words, and lives in kind deeds. Where a minister is properly esteemed and loved, there will be the greatest deference for his opinions, the most delicate attention to his comfort, a scrupulous respect for his character. Some people treat their minister as if he could feel nothing but blows. They are rude, uncourteous, churlish. Instead of this, let him see the most studious and constant care to promote his happiness and usefulness. When he is in sickness, visit him; in trouble, sympathize with him; when absent from home, take a kind interest in his family; when he returns, greet him with a smile; at the close of the labours of the Sabbath, let the deacons and leading members gather round him in the vestry, and not suffer him to retire from his scene of public labours without the reward of some tokens of their

---

* It is surprising to me that an attempt should have been made to found on no other basis than this passage, a double office of eldership in the church, and to establish a distinction between *ruling* and *preaching* elders, when nothing more can be fairly inferred from the passage, than that the apostles intended to show the whole design and duties of the elder's office, and to pronounce *him* entitled to peculiar respect, who fulfilled them all, and who to ruling well added much diligence in preaching the word.

approbation, if it be only one friendly pressure of the hand. Let him see that his prayers, and sermons, and solicitude, render him dear to the hearts of his flock. It is astonishing what an influence is sometimes produced upon a minister's mind and comfort, even by the least expression of his people's regard. Of this we have a beautiful instance in the life of St. Paul. On that important journey to Rome, which was to decide the question of life or death, he appears to have felt a season of temporary depression when the imperial city presented itself to his view. In silent meditation he revolved, not without some degree of dismay, his approaching appeal to a tribunal from which he had nothing in the way of clemency to expect. For a little while the heroism of this exalted man was somewhat affected by his situation. At this juncture, some of the Roman Christians, who had been apprized of his approach, came out as far as the Apiiforum, and the Three Taverns, to meet him, " whom, when Paul saw, he thanked God, and took courage." From that moment, fears of Nero, of prison, and of death, all left him. He sprung forward with new ardour in his career, prepared to offer himself in sacrifice on the altar of martyrdom. If, then, the love of these brethren, who had travelled a few stages to meet St. Paul, produced so happy an effect upon the mind of this illustrious apostle, how certainly might the members of our churches calculate upon a similar influence being produced upon the hearts of their pastors, by even the smaller expressions of their affection!

III. *Attendance upon their ministration*, is another duty which church members owe their pastors.

This attendance should be *constant*, not occasional. Some of our members give unspeakable pain to their pastors by the irregularity of their visits to the

house of God. A little inclemency of weather, or
the slightest indisposition of body, is sure to render
their seats vacant. Sometimes a still more guilty
cause than this exists. Oh! "Tell it not in Gath,
publish it not in Askelon, lest the daughters of the
Philistines triumph." Many professors do not scruple to devote a part of the Sabbath to *travelling*.
They do not probably set off upon a journey in the
morning of the Sabbath, and travel all day, but they
set off perhaps on Saturday evening, and arrive at
home late on Sunday morning; or they leave home
after tea on Sunday evening, and thus take only a
part of the hallowed day from its destined purpose.
This practice, it is to be feared, has much increased
of late, and is become one of the prevailing sins of
the religious world. Such persons deserve to be
brought under the censures of the church.

Some persons are irregular in their attendance
through the *distance at which they live from their
place of public worship.* Oftentimes this is unavoidable ; but it is a great inconsistency for professing
Christians voluntarily to choose a residence which,
from its remoteness from the house of God, must often deprive them of the communion of the saints.
Such a disposition to sacrifice spiritual privileges to
mere temporal enjoyment, does not afford much evidence that religion is with them the one thing needful, or that they have the mind of David, who
thought the threshold of the sanctuary was to be
preferred to the saloon and the park of the palace.
Injurious as the practice necessarily must be to the
individuals themselves, it is still more so to their
servants and children.

In the families of the poor, and in others, indeed,
where no servant is kept, the mother is detained
from public worship far more than she ought to be,

in consequence of her husband not taking his share of parental duty. Many fathers will suffer their wives to be kept from the sanctuary for weeks together, rather than take charge of their children, even for one part of the Sabbath. This is most unkind, and most unjust. A mother, it might be thought, has pain and toil enough already, without being called to suffer unnecessary privations in religious matters. That must be an unfeeling husband, who would not gladly afford an hour's rest and respite to his wife, on the day set apart for sacred repose.

Professing Christians should feel the obligations to attend *week day services.* Most ministers have often to complain, that they are 'half deserted on these occasions. Surely, with such hearts and amidst such circumstances as ours, it is too long to go from Sabbath to Sabbath without the aid of public worship. All persons have not the command of their own time; but in the case of those who have, the neglect is inexcusable, and argues a very low state of religion in the soul. And what shall be said of those members whom their pastor, on his way to the house of God, either meets going to parties of pleasure, or sees in the very circles of gayety?

A minister has a right to expect his members at the meetings for *social prayer.** The Christian that

---

* Unfortunately for the interests of our prayer meetings, some brethren who lead our devotions are so outrageously long, that after enjoying the first half of their prayers, the congregation are anxiously waiting for the close of the other half. We are often prayed into a good frame, and then prayed out of it again, by those who extend their supplications to the length of twenty or five and twenty minutes at a time. A prayer on these occasions should rarely exceed *ten minutes.* I do most earnestly

neglects these betrays such an utter indifference to
the interests of the church, and the comfort of the
pastor, as well as so much lukewarmness in his own
personal religion, as to be a fit subject for the exercise of *discipline.*

IV. *Earnest prayer.*

How often and how earnestly did the great
apostle of the Gentiles repeat that sentence, which
contained at once the authority of a command and
the tenderness of a petition—"Brethren, pray for
us." In another place, he ascribes his deliverance
and preservation to the prayers of the churches—
"You also helping together by prayer for us." 2
Cor. i. 11. Surely, then, if this illustrious man was
dependent upon, and indebted to the prayers of
Christians, how much more so the ordinary ministers
of Christ! Pray, then, for your ministers; for the
increase of their intellectual attainments, spiritual

---

recommend this to the consideration of those brethren who are
in the habit of engaging in public prayer. Devotion ends
when weariness begins. Brevity, fervour, and variety, are the
qualities which all should seek. It is also to be regretted that
the prayers are so much *alike in the arrangement of their
parts.* Each individual seems to think it necessary that he
should pursue a regular routine. How much more edifying
would it be, if one were to confine himself to one topic, and
the next were to enlarge on what the preceding one had omitted. If a person feels his mind impressed and drawn out by
any particular subject, let him confine himself to that subject,
and not suppose that his supplications will be unacceptable
either to God or man because he has not brought in the sick,
the church, the minister, the nation, the world, &c. &c. How
affecting and impressive would it be to hear a brother sometimes confine his whole intercession to his minister's usefulness;
sometimes to the church; sometimes to the spread of the gospel in the world! See a most admirable letter of Mr. Newton's
on this subject in his Omicron.

qualifications, and ministerial success. Pray for them in your private approaches to the throne of grace ; pray for them at the family altar ; and thus teach your servants and children to respect and love them. Reasons both numerous and cogent enforce this duty. It is enjoined by divine authority. It is due to the arduous nature of their employment. Little do our churches know the number and magnitude of our temptations, discouragements, difficulties, and trials.

> " 'Tis not a cause of small import
> The pastor's care demands,
> But what might fill an angel's heart,
> And filled a Saviour's hands."

Our office is no bed of down or of roses, on which the indolent may repose with careless indifference, or uninterrupted slumbers. Far, very far from it. Cares of oppressive weight; anxieties which can be known only by experience; labours of a mental kind almost too strong and incessant for the powers of mind to sustain, fall to our lot, and demand the prayerful sympathy of our flocks. And then, as another claim for our people's prayers, we might urge the consideration of their own interest, which is identified with all *our* efforts. We are to our people just what God makes us, and no more ; and he is willing to make us almost what they ask. A regard to their own spiritual profit, if nothing else, should induce them to bear us much on their hearts before the throne of divine grace. Prayer is a means of assisting a minister within the reach of all. They who can do nothing more, can pray. The *sick*, who cannot encourage their minister by their presence in the sanctuary, can bear him upon their hearts in their lonely chamber: the *poor*, who cannot add to his temporal comfort by pecuniary donations, can supplicate their God " to supply all his needs according to his riches in glory by Christ Jesus :" the *timid*, who cannot approach to offer him the tribute of their gratitude, can pour their praises into the ear of Jehovah, and entreat him still to encourage the soul of his servant: the *ignorant*, who cannot hope to add one idea to the stock of his knowledge, can place him by prayer before the fountain of celestial radiance : even the *dying*, who can no longer busy themselves as aforetime for his interests, can gather up their remaining strength, and employ it in the way of prayer for their pastor.

Prayer, if it be sincere, always increases our affection for its object. We never feel even our dearest friends to be so dear, as when we have commended them to the goodness of God. It is the best extinguisher of enmity, and the best fuel for the flame of love. If some professing Christians were to take from the time they spend in *praising* their ministers, and others from that which they employ in *blaming* them, and both were to devote it to the act of praying for them, the former would find still more cause for admiration, and the latter far less reason for censure.

V. Members *should encourage others to attend upon the ministry of their pastors.*

Let *us* go up to the house of the Lord, is an invitation which they should often address to the people of the world, who either attend no place of worship at all, or where the truth is not preached. A minister cannot himself ask people to attend his place of worship, but those who are in the habit of hearing him can; and it is astonishing to what an extent the usefulness of private Christians may be carried in this way. I have received very many into the fellowship of the church under my care, who were first brought under the sound of the gospel by the kind solicitations of a pious neighbour *To draw away the hearers of one faithful preacher to another*, is a despicable ambition—mere sectarian zeal: but to invite those who never hear the gospel, to listen to the joyful sound, is an effort worthy the mind of an angel. Shall sinners invite one another to iniquity—to the brothel, the theatre, the tavern— and Christians not attempt to draw them to the house of God? This is one way in which every member, of every church, may be the means of doing great good; the rich, the poor, male and female, masters and servants, young and old, have all some acquaintance over whom they may exert their influence; and how can it be better employed than in attracting them to those places

> " Where streams of heavenly mercy flow,
> And words of sweet salvation sound?"

VI. It is incumbent on church members *to make known to their pastor any thing of importance that occurs within the scope of their observation, or the course of their experience, relating to his church and congregation.*

For instance, their own spiritual embarrassments, trials, temptations; the declensions, backslidings, and sins of others, which they imagine may have escaped his notice, and which they have first tried, by their own personal efforts, to remove. If they perceive any root of bitterness growing up, which they have not strength or skill enough to eradicate, it is then manifestly their duty to inform him of the circumstance. If they perceive any individual whose case has been overlooked, any one in circumstances which need sympathy or relief, any who are struggling with affliction, but are too modest or timid to disclose their situation; they should bring all such occurrences under his notice. Especially should they *encourage, by their own personal attentions, any persons in the congregation who appear to be under religious concern;* in such cases, they should put forth all their tenderest solicitude to shelter and cherish these hopeful beginnings, and introduce the subjects of them to their minister. There are some Christians—but do they indeed deserve the name? —who would see all the process of conversion going on in the very next seat to theirs, and observe the fixed attention, the anxious look, the tearful eye, the serious deportment—and all this repeated one Sabbath after another—without the least possible interest, or ever exchanging a single syllable with the inquiring penitent! Shame, shame on such professors! Can the love of Christ dwell in such cold and careless hearts? Can *they* have ever felt conviction of sin? How easy and how incumbent is it to introduce ourselves to such individuals; a word, a look, would be received with gratitude.

I am aware that the part of a member's duty, enforced under this division of the subject, requires extreme caution and delicacy, not to degenerate into a busy, meddling, officious disposition. All impertinent obtrusion, all fawning activity, should be carefully avoided by the people, and as carefully discouraged by the pastor.

VII. *Zealous co-operation in all schemes of usefulness proposed by the pastor, whether for the benefit of their own society in particular, or the welfare of the church, and the world at large, is the duty of Christians.*

This is an age of restless activity, practical benevolence, and progressive improvement. One scheme of benefit often contains the germs of many more. The love of innovation and the dread of it, are equally remote from true wisdom. Zeal, when guided by wisdom, is a noble element of character, and the source of incalculable good. A church ought always to stand ready to support any scheme which is proved to their judgment to be beneficial either to themselves or others. It is most disheartening to ministers, to find all their efforts counteracted by that ignorance which can comprehend nothing strange, that bigotry which is attached to every thing old, by that timidity which starts at every thing new, or by that avarice which condemns every thing expensive. Usages and customs that are venerable for their antiquity, I admit, should not be touched by hot spirits and rude hands, lest, in removing the sediment deposited by the stream of time at the base of the fabric, they should touch the foundation itself: but where the word of God is the line and the plummet; where this line is held by the hand of caution, and watched by the eye of wisdom; in such cases, innovation upon the customs of our churches is a blessing, and ought to receive the support of the people. It is a scandal to any Christian society, when the flame of ministerial zeal is allowed to burn, without enkindling a similar fire.

VIII. *A most delicate and tender regard for the pastor's reputation.*

A minister's character is the lock of his strength; and if once this be sacrificed, he is, like Samson shorn of his hair, a poor, feeble, faltering creature, the pity of his friends and the derision of his enemies. I would not have bad ministers screened, nor would I have good ones maligned. When a preacher of righteousness has stood in the way of sinners, and walked in the counsel of the ungodly, he should never again open his lips in the great congregation, until his repentance is as notorious as his sin. But while his character is unsullied, his friends should preserve it with as much care against the tongue of the slanderer, as they would his life against the hand of the assassin.

When I consider the restless malignity of the great enemy of God and holiness, and add to this his subtlety and craft; when I consider how much his malice would be gratified, and his schemes promoted, by blackening the character of the ministers of the gospel; when I consider what a multitude of creatures there are who are his vassals, and under his influence, creatures so destitute of moral principle, and so filled with venomous spite against religion, as to be prepared to go any lengths in maligning the righteous, and especially their ministers, I can account for it on no other ground than that of a special interposition of Providence, that the reputation of Christian pastors is not more frequently attacked by slander, and destroyed by calumny. But probably we see in this, as in other cases, that wise arrangement of Providence by which things of delicacy and consequence are preserved, by calling forth greater solicitude for their safety. Church members should therefore be tremblingly alive to the importance of defending their minister's character. They should neither expect to see him perfect, nor hunt after his imperfections. When they cannot but see his imperfections—imperfections which, after all, may be consistent with not only real, but eminent piety—they should not take pleasure in either magnifying or looking at them; but make all reasonable excuse for them, and endeavour to lose sight of his infirmities in his virtues, as they do the spots of the sun amidst the blaze of radiance

with which they are surrounded.   Let them not be
the subject of conversation even between yourselves, much less before your children, servants,
and the world.   If *you* talk of his faults in derision,
who will speak of his excellences with admiration ?
Do not look at him with *suspicion*, but repose an
honourable confidence in his character.   Do not
make him an offender for a word, and refuse to him
that charity and candour of judgment, which would
be granted to every one else.   Do not magnify in-
discretions into immoralities, and exact from him
that absolute perfection, which in your own case
you find to be unattainable.   Beware of whispers,
inuendoes, significant nods, and that slanderous silence, which is more defamatory than the broadest
accusation.

Defend him against the groundless attacks of others.
Never hear him spoken of with undeserved reproach,
without indignantly repelling the shafts of calumny.
Express your firm and dignified displeasure against
the witling that would make him ridiculous, the
scorner that would render him contemptible, and
the defamer that would brand him as immoral.

Especially guard against those creeping reptiles
which infest our churches, and are perpetually insinuating that their ministers do not preach the
gospel, merely because they do not incessantly repeat the same truths in the same words ; because
they do not allegorize and spiritualize all the facts
of the Old Testament, until they have found as
much gospel in the horses of Pharaoh's chariot as
they can in St. Paul's epistles ; and because they
have dared to enforce the moral law as the rule of
the believer's conduct.   This antinomian spirit has
become the pest of many churches.   It is the most
mischievous and disgusting of all errors.   If the

heresies which abound in the spiritual world were to be represented by the noxious animals of the natural world, we could find some errors that would answer to the vulture, the tiger, and the serpent; but we could find nothing that would be an adequate emblem of antinomianism, except, by a creation of our own, we had united in some monstrous reptile, the venom of the wasp, with the deformity of the spider, and the slime of the snail.

IX. *Liberal support.*

The Scripture is very explicit on this head: "Let him that is taught in the word communicate unto him that teacheth in all good things." Gal. vi. 6. "Who goeth a warfare any time at his own charges? —even so hath the Lord ordained, that they which preach the gospel, should live of the gospel." 1 Cor. ix. 7, 14. The necessity of this appears from the injunctions delivered to ministers to devote themselves exclusively to the duties of their office." 2 Tim. ii. 4. 1 Tim. iv. 13, 15. I by no means contend that it is unlawful for a minister to engage in secular concerns; for necessity is a law which supersedes the ordinary rules of human conduct: And what are they to do, whose stipend is too small to support a family, and who have no private source of supply? A minister is under additional obligations to provide for things honest, not only in the sight of the Lord, but of men; to owe no man any thing, to provide for his own house; and if he is not enabled to do this by the liberality of his flock, and has no private fortune, he must have recourse to the labour of his hands. It is to the deep, and wide, and endless reproach of some churches, that, although possessed of ability to support their pastors in comfort, they dole out but a wretched pittance from their affluence, leaving them to make up the deficiency by a school; and then, with insulting cruelty, complain that their sermons are very meagre, and have a great sameness. Such congregations, if they were treated as they deserve, would be put upon abstinence for at least a twelve month, or until they were willing to support their pastor in comfort. They love him dearly with their lips, but hate him as cordially with their pockets. They keep him poor to keep him humble, forgetting that as humility is no less necessary for themselves than for him, this is an argument why the articles which minister to *their* pride, should be retrenched in order to support his comfort. This is certainly not drawing them with the cords of love and the bands of a man, but treating them like animals who are tamed into submission by hunger, and kept humble by being kept poor. It is curious to hear how some persons will entreat of God to bless their minister in his basket and his store, while alas! poor man, they have taken care that his basket should be empty, and his store nothingness itself. Is not this mocking both God and his minister with a solemn sound upon a thoughtless tongue?

Many rich Christians spend more in the needless wine they individually drink, than they contribute towards the support of their pastor; and others give more for the sugar that sweetens their tea, than they do for all the advantages of public worship. A reproach of this kind yet rests upon multitudes, which it is high time should be rolled away.

It is extremely difficult, where a matter of this kind must be left to voluntary contribution, and the dictates of individual liberty, to lay down particular rules; all that can be done, is, to state general principles, and leave these to operate in particular cases. Let all Christians therefore consider what

6

is a just and generous reward for the labours of a man, who is devoting his life to assist them in obtaining an inheritance incorruptible, undefiled, and that fadeth not away ; an exceeding great and eternal weight of glory :—who, in assisting them to gain eternal life, exerts at the same time an indirect, but a beneficial influence upon all their temporal prosperity—who, by his ministrations, soothes their cares, lightens their sorrows, mortifies their sins, throws a radiance over their darkest scenes, and gilds their brightest ones with additional splendour—who brings heaven down to earth for their comfort, and elevates them from earth to heaven; and who, after mitigating for them the ills of time with an anticipation of the joys of eternity, is prepared to attend them to the verge of the dark valley, and irradiate its gloom with the visions of immortality.

Let it not be thought that what is given to a minister is a *charitable donation;* it is the payment of a just debt. It is what Christ claims for his faithful servants, and which cannot be withheld without robbery. I spurn for myself and for my brethren, the degrading apprehension that we are supported by charity. We are not clerical pensioners upon mere bounty. Our appeal is to justice ; and if our claims are denied on this ground, we refuse to plead before any other tribunal, and refer the matter to the great assize.*

---

* Since the first edition of this work was printed, the author has received a letter from a very valuable and much respected deacon of his own church, which is justly entitled to the most serious attention, an extract from which is here inserted.

" MY DEAR SIR,

" I intimated to you that I should probably take the liberty to suggest to you an idea or two upon a subject which you have considered in your ' Church Member's Guide ;' and I feel

CHAPTER VI.

DUTIES OF CHURCH MEMBERS TOWARDS EACH OTHER.

1. THE first, and that which indeed seems to include every other, is LOVE.

The stress which is laid on this in the Word of God, both as it respects the manner in which it is stated, and the frequency with which it is enjoined, sufficiently proves its vast importance in the Christian temper, and its powerful influence on the communion

---

persuaded you will not attribute my suggestions to any improper motive, or deem me " intruding into those things which I ought not."

The subject is that of a minister's support. You know, Sir, that it is a principle which I have on several occasions inculcated; and the more I think of it, the more I am convinced of its perfect accordance with the law of equity, ' That it is the duty of *every* person connected with a congregation to contribute somewhat towards the support of the gospel in his own place of worship.'

The principle which I now lay down I consider to be of *universal* obligation, and applying as much to the domestic servant and to the poor man in his cottage, as to the more affluent members of our congregation. I am quite aware how difficult it is for ministers to bring this subject before their hearers, and how few are those occasions, when, consistently with delicacy and propriety, such a topic can be urged; but I do think your 'Guide' affords one of the most suitable opportunities of urging it, and its extensive circulation will, I think, bring the matter fairly before the view of the religious public. I verily believe that if all the members of our *congregations*—for I confine it not to *church members*—were to act on the principle I have laid down, and every man to do his duty, not only would the evil you justly deplore cease to exist, but a much more general effort of diffusive benevolence be the result.

Yours, very affectionately,   J. P.'

of believers. It is enforced by our Lord as the
identifying law of his kingdom. "This is my commandment, that ye love one another as I have loved
you." John xv. 12. By this we learn that the
subjects of Christ are to be known and distinguished amongst men, by their mutual affection. This
injunction is denominated *the new commandment* of
the Christian economy; not that love was no duty
before the coming of Christ; but it is now placed
more prominently amongst the duties of believers;
is urged on fresh grounds, enforced by a more perfect example, and constrained by stronger motives.
The dispensation of Jesus Christ is a system of most
wonderful, most mysterious grace; it is the manifestation, commendation, and perfection of divine
love. It originated in the love of the Father, and
is accomplished by the love of the Son. Jesus
Christ was an incarnation of love in our world. He
was love living, breathing, speaking, acting, amongst
men. His birth was the nativity of love, his sermons
the words of love, his miracles the wonders of love,
his tears the meltings of love, his crucifixion the
agonies of love, his resurrection the triumph of love.
Hence it was natural, that love should be the car-
dinal virtue in the character of his saints, and that
it should be the law which regulates their conduct
towards each other.

And it is worthy of remark, that He has made
his love to us, not only the motive, but the pattern
of our love to each other. This is my commandment, that ye love one another *as* I have loved you,
John xv. 17. Let us for our instruction dwell upon
the properties of his love, that we might know what
should be the characteristics of our own. *His* was
real and *great* affection, and not a mere nominal
one : so let us love, not in word and in tongue only,

but also in deed and in truth. *His* was *free* and *disinterested,* without any regard to our deserts : so ours should be independent of any regard to our own advantage. *His* was fruitful unto tears, and agonies, and blood, and death : so should ours in every thing that can establish the comfort of each other. *His* was a love of *forbearance* and *forgiveness :* so should ours be. *His* was purely a *spiritual* flame ; not loving them as rational creatures merely, but as objects of divine affection, and subjects of divine likeness. *His* was *unchangeable* notwithstanding our weaknesses and unkindnesses : thus are we bound to love one another, and continue unalterable in our affection to each other, in opposition to all those little infirmities of temper and conduct which we daily discover in our fellow Christians.

The Apostles echoed the language of their Master, and continually enjoined the churches which they had planted, to love one another, and to let brotherly love abound and increase. It is a grace so important that, like holiness, no measure of it is sufficient to satisfy the requirement of the Word of God. It is the basis, and cement, and beauty of the Christian union. The church where it is wanting, whatever may be the number or gifts of its members, is nothing better than a heap of stones, which, however polished, want the coherence and similitude of a palace.

In the best and purest ages of the church, this virtue shone so brightly in the character of its members, was so conspicuous in all their conduct, was expressed in actions so replete with noble, disinterested, and heroic affection, as to become a proverb with surrounding pagans, and call forth the well known exclamation, " See how these Christians love one another !" A finer eulogium was never pronounced on the Christian church; a more valuable tribute was never deposited on the altar of Christianity. Alas! that it should so soon have ceased to be just, and that the church, as it grew older, should have lost its loveliness by losing its love.

But it will be necessary to point out the manner in which brotherly love, wherever it exists, will operate.

1. *In a peculiar complacency in our fellow members, viewed as the objects of divine love.*

Complacency is the very essence of love; and the ground of all proper complacency in the saints, is their relation and likeness to God. We should feel peculiar delight in each other as fellow heirs of the grace of God; partakers of like precious faith, and joint sharers of the common salvation. We must be dear to each other as the objects of the Father's mercy, of the Son's dying grace, and of the Spirit's sanctifying influence. The love of Christians is of a very sacred nature, and is quite peculiar. It is not the love of consanguinity, or friendship, or interest, or general esteem; but it is an affection cherished for Christ's sake. They may see many things in each other to admire, such as an amiable temper, public spirit, tender sympathy; but Christian love does not rest on these things, although they may increase it, but on the ground of a common relationship to Christ. On *this account* they are to take peculiar delight in each other, as being one in Christ. "These," should a believer exclaim, as he looks on the church, "are the objects of the Redeemer's living and dying love, whom he regards with complacency; and out of affection to him, I feel an inexpressible delight in them. I love to associate with them, to talk with them, to look upon them, because they are Christ's."

2. Love to our brethren will lead us *to bear one
another's burthens, and so fulfil the law of Christ*
Gal. vi. 2.

When we see them oppressed with a weight of
anxious care, instead of carrying ourselves with
cold indifference and unfeeling distance towards
them, we should cherish a tender solicitude to know
and relieve their anxieties. How touching would
such a salutation as the following be, from one
Christian to another: " Brother, I have observed,
with considerable pain, that your countenance has
been covered with gloom, as if you were sinking
under some inward solicitude. I would not be
unpleasantly officious, nor wish to obtrude myself
upon your attention, farther than is agreeable ; but
I offer you the expressions of Christian sympathy,
and the assistance of Christian counsel. Can I in
any way assist to mitigate your care, and restore
your tranquillity ?" At such sounds, the loaded
heart would feel as if half its load were gone. It
may be, the kind inquirer could yield no effectual
relief; but there is balm in his sympathy. The indifference of some professing Christians to the
burthens of their brethren is shocking ; they would
see them crushed to the very earth with cares and
sorrows, and never make one kind inquiry into their
situation, nor lend a helping hand to lift them from
the dust. Love requires that we should take the
deepest interest in each other's case, that we should
patiently listen to the tale of wo which a brother
brings us, that we should mingle our tears with his,
that we should offer him our advice, that we should
suggest to him the consolations of the gospel ; in
short, we should let him see that his troubles reach
not only our ear, but our heart. Sympathy is one

of the finest, the most natural, the most easy expressions of love.

3. Love requires that *we should visit our brethren in their affliction.*

" I was sick and ye visited me, I was in prison and ye came unto me ;—for as much as ye did it unto the least of these my brethren, ye did it unto me ;" such is the language of Jesus Christ to his people, by which he teaches us how important and incumbent a duty it is for church members to visit each other in their afflictions. Probably there is no duty more neglected than this.   Christians often lie on beds of sickness for weeks and months successively, without seeing a fellow member cross the threshold of their chamber door.   How often have I been shocked, when upon inquiring of the sufferer whether such and such an individual residing in their neighbourhood had been to visit them, it had been said in reply, " Oh! no, sir, I have now been stretched on this bed for days and weeks.   My pain and weakness have been so great, that I have scarcely been able to collect my thoughts for meditation and prayer.   The sight of a dear Christian friend would indeed have relieved the dull monotony of this gloomy scene, and the voice of piety would have been as music to blunt my sense of pain, and lull my troubled heart to short repose ; but such a sight and such a sound have been denied me.   No friend has been near me, and it has aggravated sorrows, already heavy, to be thus neglected and forgotten by a church, which I joined with the hope of finding amongst them the comfort of sympathy.   But alas! alas! I find them too much occupied with the things seen and temporal, to think of a suffering brother, to whom wearisome nights and months of vanity are appointed." How could I help exclaiming, "O, Christian love, bright image of the Saviour's heart! whither hast thou fled, that thou so rarely visitest the church on earth, to shed thine influence, and manifest thy beauties there?" There have been ages of Christianity—so historians inform us—in which brotherly love prevailed amongst Christians to such a degree, that, fearless of the infection diffused by the most malignant and contagious disorders, they have ventured to the bed side of their brethren expiring in the last stages of the plague, to administer the consolations of a hope full of immortality. This *was* love ; love stronger than death, and which many waters could not quench. It was no doubt imprudent, but it was heroic, and circulated far and wide the praises of that dear name which was the secret of the wonder.

How many are there, now bearing the Christian name, who scarcely ever yet paid one visit to the bed side of a suffering brother! Shame and disgrace upon such professors!! Let *them* not expect to hear the Saviour say, "I was sick and *ye* visited me."

That this branch of Christian love may be performed with greater diligence, it would be a good plan for the pastor, at every church meeting, to mention the names of the afflicted members, and stir up the brethren to visit them. It would be particularly desirable for Christians to go to the scene of suffering on a Sabbath day, and read the Bible and sermons to the afflicted, at that time, as they are then peculiarly apt to feel their sorrows, in consequence of being cut off from the enjoyments of public worship.

4. "*Pray one for another,*" James v. 16.

Not only *with*, but *for* one another. A Christian

7

should take the interests of his brethren into the closet. Private devotion is not to be selfish devotion. It would much increase our affection did we devote more of our private prayers to each other's welfare.

5. *Pecuniary relief should be administered to those who need it.*

"Distributing to the necessities of the saints," Rom. xii. 13, is mentioned amongst the incumbent duties of professing Christians. How just, how forcible is the interrogation of the Apostle, 1 John iii. 17, "Whoso hath this world's good, and seeth his brother have need, and shutteth up his bowels of compassion from him, how dwelleth the love of God in him?" Nothing can be more absurd than those pretensions to love, which are not supported by exertions to relieve the wants of the object beloved. It must be a singular affection which is destitute of mercy. So powerfully did this holy passion operate in the first ages of the church, that many rich Christians sold their estates, and shared their affluence with the poor. What rendered this act the more remarkable is, that it was purely voluntary. It is not *our duty* any more than it was theirs, to go this length; still, however, it is evident both from general principles as well as from particular precepts, that we are under obligation to make some provision for the comfort of the poor. This duty must be left in the statement of general terms, as it is impossible to define its precise limits. It does not appear to me to be at all incumbent to make regular periodical distributions to the poor, whether in circumstances of distress or not. Some churches have a registered list of pensioners, who come as regularly for their pay, as if they were hired servants. If they are old, infirm, or unprovided for, this is very well; but for those to receive relief, who are getting a comfortable subsistence by their labour, is an abuse of the charity of the church. The money collected at the Lord's supper, should be reserved for times of sickness and peculiar necessity.

It should be recollected, also, that *public* contributions do not release the members from the exercise of *private liberality*. The shilling a month which is given at the sacrament, seems, in the opinion of many, to discharge them from all further obligation to provide for the comfort of their poorer brethren, and to be a sort of composition for the full exercise of religious charity. This is a great mistake; it ought rather to be considered as a mere earnest, or pledge of all that more effective and abundant liberality which they should exercise in secret. Every Christian who is indulged with a considerable share of the bounties of Providence ought to consider the poorer members of the church, who may happen to live in his neighbourhood, as the objects of his *peculiar* care, interest, and relief.

6. *Forbearance is a great part of love.*

"Forbearing one another in love." Eph. iv. 2. In a Christian church, especially where it is of considerable magnitude, we must expect to find a very great diversity of character. There are all the gradations of intellect, and all the varieties of temper. In such cases, great forbearance is absolutely essential to the preservation of harmony and peace. The strong must bear with the infirmities of the weak. Christians of great attainments in knowledge should not in their hearts despise, nor in their conduct ridicule, the feeble conceptions of those who are babes in Christ; but most meekly correct their errors, and most kindly instruct their ignorance. This is love. In very many persons there will unhappily be found

some things, which, although they by no means affect the reality and sincerity of their religion, considerably diminish its lustre, and have a tendency,
without the caution of love, to disturb our communion with them. Some have a forward and obtrusive manner; others are talkative; others indulge
a complaining, whining, begging disposition; others
are abrupt, almost to rudeness, in their address.
These, and many more, are the spots of God's children—with which we are sometimes so much dis-
pleased, as to feel an alienation of heart from the
subjects of them, although we have no doubt of their
real piety. Now here is room for the exercise of
love. These are the cases in which we are to employ that charity which covereth all things. Are
we to love only amiable Christians? Perhaps, after
all, in the substantial parts of religion, these rough
characters far excel others, whom courtesy and
amiableness have carried to the highest degree of
polish. I do not say we are to love these individuals *for* their peculiarities, but *in spite* of them.
Not on their own account, but for Christ's sake, to
whom they belong. And what can be a greater
proof of our affection for him, than to love an un-
lovely individual on his account?

If you had the picture of a valued friend, would
you withdraw from it your affection, and throw it
away, because there was a spot upon the canvass,
which in some degree disfigured the painting? No:
you would say, it is a likeness of my friend still,
and I love it, notwithstanding its imperfection. The
believer is a picture of your best friend; and will
you discard him, neglect him, because there is a
speck upon the painting?

7. *Love should induce us to watch over one
another.*

Am I my brother's keeper? was an inquiry suitable enough in the lips of a murderer, but most unsuitable and inconsistent from a Christian.   We
are brought into fellowship for the very purpose of
being keepers of each other.   We are to watch
over our brethren, and admonish and reprove them
as circumstances may require.   I do not mean that
church members should pry into each other's secrets, or be busy bodies in other men's matters, for
that is forbidden by God and abominable in the sight
of man. 1 Thess. iii. 11. 1 Pet. iv. 15.   Much less
are they to assume authority over each other, and
act the part of proud and tyrannical inquisitors.
But still we are to " exhort one another daily, lest
any be hardened through the deceitfulness of sin."
We are not to suffer sin to be committed, or duty
to be omitted by a brother, without affectionately
admonishing him.   What can be more incumbent,
more obligatory, than this?   Can we indeed love
any one, and at the same time see him do that which
we know will injure him, without entreating him
to desist?   " Brethren, if any man be overtaken in
a fault, ye which are spiritual restore such an one
in the spirit of meekness." Gal. vi. 1.

Let us then take heed against that Cain-like
spirit which is too prevalent in our churches, and
which leads many to act as if their fellow-members
were no more to them than the stranger at the ends
of the earth.   Striking are the words of God to the
Jews, " Thou shalt not hate thy brother in thy heart;
thou shalt in any wise rebuke him, and not suffer
sin upon him." Lev. xix. 17. Not to rebuke him,
then, when he sins, is, instead of loving him, to hate
him.   This neglect is what the apostle means by
being partakers of other men's sins.   The admonition to " warn the unruly," 1 Thess. v. 14. was de-

livered not merely to ministers, but to private Christians.

I know no duty more neglected than this. It is one of the most prevailing defects of Christians. Many a backslider would have been prevented from going far astray, if, in the very first stages of his declension, some brother, who had observed his critical state, had faithfully and affectionately warned and admonished him. What shame, and anguish, and disgrace, would the offender himself have been spared, and what dishonour and scandal would have been averted from the church, by this one act of faithful love!

I am aware it is a difficult and self-denying duty; but that cannot excuse its neglect. Love will enable us to perform it, and the neglect of it violates the law of Christ.

II. Church members should cultivate PEACE and HARMONY one with another.

"Keep the unity of the Spirit in the bond of peace. Ephes. iv. 3. Be of one mind, live in peace. 2 Cor. iii. 11. Follow after the things which make for peace. Rom. xiv. 19." It is quite needless to expatiate on the value and importance of peace. What society can exist without it? I shall therefore proceed to state what things are necessary for the attainment of this end.

1. *Members should be subject one to another in humility.* "Likewise, ye younger, submit yourselves unto the elder. Yea, all of you, be subject one to another, and be clothed with humility." 1 Pet. v. 5. Now from hence we learn, that some kind of mutual subjection ought to be established in every Christian church. This of course does not mean, that some members are to make an entire surrender of their opinions and feelings to others, so far as

never to oppose them, and always to be guided by
them. It is not the subjection of an inferior to a
superior, but of equals to one another; not that
which is extorted by authority, but voluntarily conceded by affection; not yielded as matter of right,
but given for the sake of peace: in short, it is the
mutual subjection of love and humility. Young
and inexperienced persons ought to be subject to
the aged; for what can be more indecorous than to
see a stripling standing up at a church meeting, and,
with confidence and flippancy, opposing his views
to those of a disciple old enough to be his grand-
father? Youth loses its loveliness when it loses its
modesty. They should hearken with deference and
most reverential attention to the opinion of the aged.
Nor does the obligation rest here; it extends to
those who are equal in age and rank. Church members should be subject to each other; they should
not be determined at all events to have their own
way, but should go as far as principle would let
them, in giving up their own views and predilections
to the rest. Every one should hearken with respectful attention to the opinions of others, and be willing to sacrifice his own. The contention ought
not to be for rule, but for subjection. Instead of
haughtily exclaiming, " I have as much right to have
my way as any one else," we should say, " I have
an opinion, and will mildly and respectfully state it;
yet I will not force it upon the church, but give way
to the superior wisdom of others, if I am opposed."
There should be in every member a supposition that
others may see as clearly, probably more so, than
himself.

The democratic principle in our system of church
government must not be stretched too far. The
idea of equal rights is soon abused, and converted

into the means of turbulence and faction. Liberty, fraternity, and equality, are words which, both in church and state, have often become the signals, in the mouths of some, for the lawless invasion of the rights of others. It has been strangely forgotten, that no man in social life has a right to please only himself; his will is, or ought to be, the good of the whole. And that individual violates at once the social compact, whether in ecclesiastical or civil society, who pertinaciously and selfishly exclaims, "I *will* have *my* way." Such a declaration constitutes him a rebel against the community. Yet, alas! how much of this rebellion is to be found not only in the world, but in the church; and what havoc and desolation has it occasioned! Unfortunately for the peace of our societies, it is sometimes disguised, by the deceitfulness of the human heart, under the cloak of zeal for the general good. Church members should enter into these sentiments, and thus comply with the apostolic admonitions, "Let nothing be done through strife or vain-glory, but in lowliness of mind let each esteem others better than themselves." Phil. ii. 3. "In honour preferring one another." Rom. xii. 10.

2. To the preservation of peace, *a right treatment of offences is essentially necessary.*

We should ever be cautious not to GIVE *offence.*

Some persons are rude, dogmatical, or indiscreet; they never consult the feelings of those around them, and are equally careless whom they please and whom they offend. They say and do just what their feelings prompt, without the least regard to the consequences of their words and actions. They act like an individual who, because it pleases him, discharges a loaded musket in a crowded street, where some are almost sure to be wounded. This

is not the charity which is kind, courteous, and civil.
A Christian should be ever afraid of giving offence;
he should be anxious not to injure the wing of an
insect, much more the mind of a brother. The
peace of his brethren should even be more sacred
than his own. It should be his fixed determination
never, if possible, to occasion a moment's pain.
For this purpose he should be discreet, and mild,
and courteous in all his language, weighing the
import of words before he utters them, and calcu-
lating the consequence of actions before he performs
them. He should remember that he is moving in
a crowd, and be careful not to trample on, or jostle
his neighbours.

We should all be backward to RECEIVE *offence.*

Quarrels often begin for want of the caution I
have just stated, and are then continued for want
of the backwardness I am now enforcing. An
observance of these two principles would keep the
world in peace. There are some people whose passions are like tow, kindled into a blaze in a moment
by the least spark which has been designedly or
accidentally thrown upon it. A word, a look, is in
some cases quite enough to be considered a very
serious injury. It is no uncommon thing for such
persons to excuse themselves on the ground that
their feelings are so delicately sensible, that they
are offended by the least touch. This is a humiliating confession, for it is acknowledging that, instead
of being like the cedar of Lebanon, or the oak of
the forest, which laughs at the tempest, and is
unmoved by the boar of the wood, they resemble
the sensitive plant, a little squeamish shrub, which
trembles before the breeze, and shrivels and contracts
beneath the pressure of an insect. Delicate feelings!! In plain English, this means that they are

petulant and irascible. I would have a text of Scripture written upon a label, and tied upon the forehead of such persons, and it should be this— " Beware of dogs."

We should never suffer ourselves to be offended, until, at least, we are sure that offence was *intended ;* and this is really not so often as we are apt to conclude. Had we but patience to wait, or humility to inquire, we should find that many things were done by mistake, which we are prone to attribute to design. How often do we violate that charity which thinketh no evil, and which imperatively demands of us to attribute a good motive to another's conduct, except a bad one is proved! Let us then deliberately determine, that, by God's grace, we will not be easily offended. If such a resolution were generally made and kept, offences would cease. Let us first ascertain whether offence was intended, before we suffer the least emotion of anger to be indulged ; and even then, when we have proved that the offence was not committed by accident, let us next ask ourselves whether it is necessary to notice it. What wise man will think it worth while, when an insect has stung him, to pursue and punish the aggressor ?

When we have received an injury which is too serious to be passed over unnoticed, and requires explanation in order to our future pleasant intercourse with the individual who inflicts it, *we should neither brood over it in silence, nor communicate it to a third person, but go directly to the offender himself, and state to him in private our views of his conduct.* This is most clearly enjoined by our divine Lord—" Moreover, if thy brother trespass against thee, go and tell him his fault between thee and him alone : if he shall hear thee, thou hast gained thy brother." Matt.

xviii. 15.   Many persons lock up the injury in their own bosom; and instead of going to their offending brother, dwell upon his conduct in silence, until their imagination has added to it every possible aggravation, and their minds have come to the conclusion to separate themselves forever from his society. From that hour, they neither speak to him, nor think well of him; but consider and treat him as an alien from their hearts.   This is not *religion*.   Our duty is to go, and to go as speedily as possible, to the offender.   The longer we delay, the more serious will the offence appear in our eyes, and the more difficult will it be to persuade ourselves to obtain the interview.

Others, when they have received an offence, *set off to some friend*, perhaps to more than one, to lodge their complaint, and tell how they have been treated.   The report of the injury spreads farther and wider, exaggerated and swelled by those circumstances, which every gossip through whose hands it passes, chooses to add to the original account, till, in process of time, it comes round to the offender himself, in its magnified and distorted form, who now finds that he, in his turn, is aggrieved and calumniated; and thus a difficult and complicated case of offence, grows out of what was at first very simple in its nature, and capable of being adjusted.   *We ought to go at once to the party offending us, before a syllable has passed our lips on the subject to a third person; and we should also close our ears against the complaints of any individual, who would inform us of the fault of a brother, before he has told the offender himself.*

Sometimes, when persons have received a supposed offence, *they will endeavour to gain information from others in a circuitous and clandestine man-*

ner, in order, as they think, to conduct the affair with prudence. This is crooked policy, and rarely succeeds. It is next to impossible to creep with a step so soft, and to speak with a voice so muffled, as to escape detection; and if the individual surprise us in the act of ferreting into holes and corners for evidence, it will be sure to excite his indignation and disgust. No, *go to him at once,* AND ALONE. This is the command of Scripture, and it is approved by reason, Matt. xviii. 15—17. This single admonition is worth all the volumes that philosophy ever wrote, and ought to be inscribed in letters of gold. It cannot be too often repeated, nor can too much stress be laid upon it. Third persons, whose ears are ever open to catch reports, should be avoided as the plague; *they* are the mischief-makers and quarrel-mongers, and are the pests of our churches.

Great caution, however, should be observed *as to the spirit in which we go to the offending brother.* All the meekness and gentleness of Christ should be in our temper and manner. We should dip our very tongue in the fountain of love. Every feeling, every look, every tone of anger, should be suppressed. We should not *at once accuse* our brother of the injury, for the report may be false; but modestly ask him if it be correct. All attempts to extort confession by threatenings should be avoided; and instead of these, nothing should be employed but the appeals of wisdom, the gentle persuasions of love.* If we succeed in this private interview to gain our brother so far as to produce a little re-

---

* There is a very interesting description of the manner in which private offences should be treated, in that inimitable book, "Social Religion Exemplified;" a book which every professing Christian ought to read, and which, having begun to read, he will never lay aside, till he has finished it. Part of a

lenting, we ought to cherish, by the kindest expressions, these beginnings of repentance, and to avoid

---

dialogue I here transcribe, as showing the manner and spirit in
which this very difficult matter ought to be managed :—

"NEOPHYTUS. If *Epenetus* please, and with the good
leave of the company, I would further request a brief account
of *private offences,* that probably occurred among these professing brethren.

"EPENETUS. I shall then gratify my young friend, which I
am persuaded will not be ungrateful to the company. Upon a
time, in some discourse which *Egwan* (of whom you have heard
something before) and one *Hyderus* had, wherein they differed
in opinion, the latter told the former that he was an *insignificant fellow,* whose thoughts were not to be regarded. *Egwan*
said in answer, that he took it very ill of him. The other replied, You may take it as you please. So their conversation
ended in a cloud. *Egwan* had but little rest that night. Is it so,
then, he says to himself; and yet did Christ redeem me? Did
the Spirit of the Lord visit my heart? Did the church of Christ
receive me? And must I (though weak and feeble) be called
insignificant? Tossed through the night in much uneasiness, he
thought to go in the morning to one of the elders to complain.
He got up, and, as usual, in the first place committed himself to
God : but while he was at prayer, mourning over his present uneasiness, that word came into his mind, *If thy brother shall trespass against thee, go and tell him his fault between thee and him
alone.* He quickly saw, that it was not his *immediate* business
to *divulge* it to any body,—no, not to an elder; but to go directly to the brother who gave him the offence. Accordingly,
he desired God to give him meekness of wisdom from above,
and to bless his design. So he went to *Hyderus,* and spoke to
him as follows ·

Egwan. Brother, I have had a very uneasy night; you
spoke, I think, very unadvisedly with your lips, to say no
worse of it ; you have grieved me much, and surely you have
sinned against God. I have judged it my duty to come and
have some talk with you about it ; and have mentioned it
to none but the Lord. You know you called me, in disdain,
An insignificant fellow. Pray, what do you think of the *expression,* and of the *spirit* in which it was spoken?

Hyderus. Truly, I think it was not worth your while to
come to me about it. I charge you not with pride ; yet pray

all demands of unnecessary concession, all haughty
airs of conscious superiority, all insulting methods

does it not look very much that way, that you should make it
your business to come hither to prove yourself valuable and
significant?

Egwan. I came with no other design than to tell you my
grievance. For if I am such a person as, with disdain, you described me, then am I not regarded by the Redeemer; have
no portion in him; nor doth his Spirit dwell in me; nor hath he
ever taken notice of me; otherwise, sure, I should be entitled
to a place in the esteem of his children. Why did the church
receive me? You have censured the whole church and its elders, as well as myself.

Hyderus. I do not pretend to justify what I said; but think
you greatly aggravate it; whereas, you might as well have
been easy without taking any notice of it.

Egwan. And suffer the sin to lie upon you? Brother, nothing is desired but repentance for sinning against God. I hope
I am willing to think *meanly* of myself, but am not so willing
that any thing appertaining to the Redeemer's kingdom should
be treated with derision or disdain.

Hyderus. Dear brother, I disdain you not; you discover
yourself to be a Christian of good improvement. I am sorry to
have so sinned against God and you, and desire that brotherly
love and tender respect may continue.

Egwan. Amen; I am satisfied, dear brother.

Christophilus. What a speedy, happy end was put to
this offence! Oh, what endless strife of tongues, evil surmisings,
animosities, and popular clamour, spring and prevail in some
places, for want of observing such a method as this!

Neophytus. But what if *Egwan* had gone to the elder *first*,
as he thought once to do?

Epenetus. Why, then he would have been reproved for
taking such a wrong step; would have been better informed,
and sent about his business.

Neophytus. But what if *Hyderus* had justified himself and
persisted in his sin?

Epenetus. Then *Egwan* must have taken another opportunity, and desired a brother or two to go along with him,
that they might use their joint endeavours to bring the offender
to repentance.

of dispensing pardon. "Brother," we should say, "my aim was not to *degrade* you, but to *convince* you; and since you see and acknowledge your fault, I am satisfied, and shall forgive and forget it from this moment."

If the offender should refuse to acknowledge his fault, and it should be necessary for us to take a witness or two, which is our next step in settling a disagreement, *we must be very careful to select men of great discretion and calmness;* men who will not be likely to inflame, instead of healing the wound; men who will act as *mediators*, not as *partisans*.

It is absolutely necessary, in order to offences being removed, that the offender, upon his being convicted of an injury, *should make all suitable concession;* and it will generally be found, that in long continued and complicated strifes, *this obligation becomes mutual.* Whoever is the ORIGINAL aggressor a feud seldom continues long, ere *both parties* are to blame. Even the aggrieved individual has something to concede; and the way to induce the other to acknowledge his greater offence, is for him to confess his lesser one. It is the mark of a noble and ingenuous mind to confess an error, and solicit its forgiveness. "Confess your faults one to another," is an inspired injunction. The man who is too proud to acknowledge his fault, when his conduct demands it, has violated his duty, and is a fit subject for censure. There are some persons, so far forgetful of their obligations to Christ and to their brethren, as not only to refuse to make concession, but even to *give explanation.* Their proud spirits disdain even to afford the least satisfaction in the way of throwing light upon a supposed offence. This is most criminal, and is such a defiance of the authority of the Lord Jesus, as ought to bring the individual before the bar of the church.

We should be very cautious *not to exact unreasonable concession.* A revengeful spirit is often as effectually gratified by imposing hard and humiliating terms of reconciliation, as it possibly could be by making the severest retaliation. No offender is so severely punished, as he who is obliged to degrade himself in order to obtain a pardon. And as all revenge is unlawful, we should be extremely careful not to gratify it at the very time and by the manner in which we are dispensing pardon. To convince a brother, not to degrade him, is the object we are to seek; and especially should we endeavour to show him, that his offence is more against Christ than against ourselves.

When suitable acknowledgments are made, *the act of forgiveness is no longer optional with us.* From that moment every spark of anger, every feeling of a revengeful nature, is to be quenched. "Let not the sun go down upon your wrath, neither give place to the devil." Ephes. iv. 26, 27. If we suffer sleep to visit our eyes before we have forgiven an offending, but penitent brother, *we* are committing a greater offence against Christ, than our brother has committed against us. The man that takes a revengeful temper to his pillow, is inviting Satan to be his guest. Such a man would probably tremble at the thought of taking a harlot to his bed; but is it no crime to sleep in the embrace of a *fiend?* The word revenge should be blotted from the Christian's vocabulary by the tears which he sheds for his own offences. How can an implacable Christian repeat that petition of our Lord's prayer, "Forgive me my trespasses *as* I forgive them that trespass against

me?" Does he forget that if he uses such language
while he is living in a state of resentment against
a brother, *he is praying for perdition?*—for how does
he forgive them that trespass against him? By revenge. How strong is the language of St. Paul!
" Grieve not the Holy Spirit of God whereby ye are
sealed unto the day of redemption. Let all bitterness, and wrath, and clamour, and evil speaking, be
put away from you, with all malice: and be kind
one to another, and tender hearted, forgiving one
another, even as God, for Christ's sake, hath forgiven you." Ephes. iv. 30—32. What motives
to a forgiving spirit!! Can that man have ever
tasted the sweets of pardoning mercy, who refuses
to forgive an erring brother? Go, Christian profess-
or, go first to the law, and learn thy twice ten
thousand sins; go in imagination to the brink of the
bottomless pit, and as thou hearkenest to the howlings of the damned, remember that those howlings
might have been thine; then go to the cross, and
while thou lookest on the bleeding victim, which is
nailed to it, hearken to the accents of mercy which
breathe like soft music in thine ear, " Go in peace,
thy sins are all forgiven thee." What, *will* you,
can you return from such scenes, with purposes of
revenge? No; impossible. An *implacable Christian* is a contradiction in terms. " Bigots there may
be, and have been, of all denominations; but an
implacable, irreconcilable, unforgiving Christian, is
of the same figure of speech, as a godly adulterer,
a religious drunkard, a devout murderer."*

The last step in reclaiming an offender, is *to bring
him before the assembled church.* " If he will not

Dr. Grosvenor's most pathetic Sermon on the "'Temper
of Jesus."

8

hear thee, then take with thee one or two more, that in the mouth of two or three witnesses, every word may be established; and if he shall neglect to hear them, tell it unto the church; but if he neglect to hear the church, let him be unto thee as a heathen man and a publican." Every effort that ingenuity can invent, affection prompt, or patience can conduct, ought to be made, before it be brought to be investigated by the brethren at large. If every trivial disagreement be laid before the church, it will soon become a court of common pleas, and have all its time consumed in adjusting matters of which it ought never to have heard. Before a public inquiry takes place, the pastor should be made acquainted with the matter; who, if he possess the confidence and affection of his people, will have sufficient influence, at least in all ordinary cases, to terminate the difference in an amicable manner. It is best to settle it even without his interference, if possible; but it is better to consult him in every case, before the affair is submitted to the last tribunal.

An offence ought never to be considered as removed, until love is restored. We should never rest until such an explanation has been given and received, as will enable us to return to harmony and confidence. A mere cessation of actual hostilities may do for the intercourse of the world, but not for the fellowship of the saints. There is no actual strife between the tenants of the sepulchre; but the cold and gloomy stillness of a church-yard is an inappropriate emblem of the peace of a Christian church. In such a community, we expect, that not only will the discords and sounds of enmity be hushed, but the sweet harmonies of love be heard; not only that the conflict of rage will terminate, but be succeeded by the activity of genuine affection.

When once an offence has been removed, it should never be adverted to in future. Its very remembrance should, if possible, be washed from the memory by the waters of Lethe. Other causes of disagreement may exist, and fresh feuds arise ; but the old one is dead and buried, and its angry ghost should never be evoked to add fury to the passion of its successor. Nor should *we*, when in our turn we are convicted of an error, shelter ourselves from reproof, by reminding our reprover, that he was once guilty of a similar offence. This is mean, dishonourable, unchristian, and mischievous.

Every Christian should bear reproof with meekness. Few know how to give reproof with propriety, still fewer how to bear it. "Let the righteous smite me, it shall be a kindness ; and let him reprove me, it shall be as excellent oil, which shall not break my head." How small is the number who can adopt this language in sincerity! What wounded pride, what mortification and resentment are felt by many when their faults are told to them. When we have so far sinned as to deserve rebuke, we ought to have humility enough to bear it with meekness; and should it be delivered in greater weight, or with less affection than we think is proper, a penitential remembrance of our offence should prevent all feelings of irritation or resentment. The scripture is very severe in its language to those who turn with neglect, anger or disgust from the admonitions of their brethren. "He that despiseth reproof sinneth." Prov. x. 17. "He that hateth reproof is brutish." Prov. xii. 1. "He that is often reproved, and yet hardeneth his neck, shall be suddenly destroyed, and that without remedy." Prov. xxix. 1. Such persons are guilty of great pride, great neglect of the word of God, and great contempt of one of the ordinances of Heaven, and thus injure their souls by that which was given to benefit them.

Do not then act so wickedly as to turn with indignation from a brother that comes in the spirit of meekness to admonish and reprove you. Rather thank him for his fidelity, and profit by his kindness. I know not a more decisive mark of true and strong piety than a willingness to receive reproof with meekness, and to profit by admonition, come from whom it might.

2. If the peace of the church be preserved, *the members must watch against and repress* A TATTLING DISPOSITION.

There are few circumstances which tend more to disturb the harmony and repose of our societies, than a proneness, in some of their members, to a gossipping, tattling disposition. There are persons so deeply infected with the Athenian passion to hear or tell some new thing, that their ears or lips are always open. With insatiable appetite they devour all the news they can by any means collect, and are never easy until it is all disgorged again, to the unspeakable annoyance and disgust of others around them. It is one of the mysteries of God's natural government, that such should gain a sort of adventitious consequence by the mischief they occasion, and be thus sheltered from scorn by being regarded with dread. The *tattler* is of this description: I mean the individual who loves to talk of other men's matters, and especially of their *faults ;* for it will be found, that by a singular perversity of disposition, those who love to talk about the circumstances of others, rarely ever select their *excellences* as matter of discourse, but almost always fix upon their *failings ;* and thus, to borrow a simile of Solomon's, they resemble the fly which neglects the healthful

part of the frame to pitch and luxuriate on the
sore.

In the case of tattling there are generally three
parties to blame; there is first the gossip, then the
person who is weak enough to listen to, and report
the tales; and lastly, the individual who is the subject of the report, who suffers his mind to be irri-
tated, instead of going, in the spirit of meekness, to
require an explanation from the original reporter.

Now let it be a rule with every church member,
*to avoid speaking of the circumstances, and especially
of the faults of others.* Let this rule have the sanctity of the laws of Heaven, and the immutability
of those of the Medes and Persians. Let every
individual resolve with himself thus: " I will be slow
to speak of others. I will neither *originate* a report
by saying what I think, nor help to *circulate* a report by repeating what I hear." This is a most
wise regulation, which would at once preserve our
own peace and the peace of society. We should
beware of saying any thing, which, by the perverted
ingenuity of a slanderous disposition, may become
the basis of a tale to the disadvantage of another.
It is not enough, as I have hinted, that we do not
originate a report, but we ought not to *circulate* it.
When it reaches us, there it should stop, and go no
farther. We should give it to prudence, to be
buried in silence. *We must never appear pleased*
with the tales of gossips and newsmongers, much
less with the scandals of the backbiter; our smile
is their reward. *If there were no listeners, there
would be no reporters.* In company, let us always
discourage and repress such conversation. Talkers
know where to find a market for their stuff; and
like poachers and smugglers, who never carry their
contraband articles to the house of an exciseman,

they never offer their reports to an individual who, they know, would reprove them in the name of Jesus.

Let us avoid and discourage the hollow, deceitful practice of indulging a tattling disposition under the cover of lamenting over the faults of our brethren.

Many who would be afraid or ashamed to mention the faults of a brother in the way of direct affirmation or report, easily find, or attempt to find, a disguise for their backbiting disposition in *affected lamentations.* " What a pity it is," they exclaim, " that brother B. should have behaved so ill.   Poor man, I am sorry that he should have committed himself.   The petulance of his temper is exceedingly to be regretted.   He does not much honour religion." " And then," replies a second, " how sorry I am to hear this report of sister C.!   How the world will talk, and the cause of Christ suffer by such unwarrantable things in the conduct of a professor!   It will not be a secret long, or I would not mention it." " Oh," says a third, " I have heard whispers of the same kind in times past.   I have long suspected it, and mentioned my fears some months ago to a friend or two.   I thought she was not the person she appeared to be.   I am very sorry for her, and for the cause of Christ.   I have long had my suspicions, and now they are all confirmed.   I shall tell the friends to whom I expressed my fears what I have now heard."   In this way is a tattling disposition indulged in the circles of even good people, under the guise of lamentation for the sins of others. " Odious and disgusting cant!" would a noble and honourable Christian exclaim, with hallowed indignation ; " which of you, if you really lamented the fact, would report it ?   Which of you has gone to the erring individual, inquired into the truth of the matter, and, finding it true, has mildly expostulated? Let your lamentations be poured out before God and the offender, but to none else."

Others, again, indulge this disposition *by running about to inquire into the truth of a report, which they say has reached them, respecting a brother.* "Have you heard any thing of brother H. lately?" they ask, with a significant look. "No," replies the person. "Then I suppose it is not true." "Why, what have you heard? Nothing, I hope, affecting his moral character." "Not *very* materially; but I hope it is false." The tattler cannot go, however, without letting out the secret, and then sets off to inquire of another and another. Mischief making creature! Why had he not gone, as was his obvious duty, to the individual who was the subject of the report, and inquired of him the truth of it? Ay, but then the story would have been contradicted at once, and the pleasure of telling it would have been ended.

There are cases in which a modest disclosure of the failings of others *is necessary.* Such, for example, as when a church is likely to be deceived in the character of an individual, whom it is about to admit to communion. In such instances, the person who is aware of the imposition that is likely to be practised, should go directly to the pastor, and make him acquainted with the fact; instead of which, some persons whisper their suspicions to any and to many, *except* the pastor. It is perfectly lawful also to prevent any brother from being betrayed into a ruinous confidence in pecuniary matters, by informing him of the character of the individual by whom he is about to be deceived. Silence, in such cases, would be an obvious injury.

BE SLOW TO SPEAK, then, is a maxim which every Christian should always keep before his eyes. Si-

lent people can do no harm ; but talkers are always
dangerous.

III. Besides these things, there are duties which
members owe to the church in its *collective* capacity.

1. They are bound *to take a deep interest in its concerns, and to seek its prosperity by all lawful means.*

Every one should feel that he has a personal
share in the welfare of the society. He should consider that, having selected that particular community
with which he is associated, as his religious home,
he is under a solemn obligation to promote, by every
proper effort, its real interest. He is to be indifferent to nothing which at any time affects its prosperity. Some members, from the moment they have
joined a Christian church, take no concern in any
of its affairs. They scarcely ever attend a church
meeting ; they know neither who are excluded, nor
who are received. If members are added, they express no delight ; if none are admitted, they feel no
grief. They fill up their places at the table of the
Lord, and in the house of God ; and beyond this,
seem to have nothing else to do with the church.
This is a most criminal apathy ; a Christian ought
to be as tremblingly alive to the welfare of the religious society to which he is united, as he is to the
success of his worldly affairs.

2. They are bound *to attend all the meetings of the
church,* at least so far as their circumstances will
allow. They had better be absent from sermons
and prayer-meetings, than from these. How can
they know the state of the society, if they are not
present when its affairs are exhibited and arranged ?
or how can they exercise that proper confidence in
the piety of the brethren, which is essential to fellowship, if they are absent at the time of their admission ?

3. *They should most conscientiously devote their
gifts, graces and abilities to the service of the church,
in an orderly and modest way;* neither obtruding
their assistance when it is not required, nor with-
holding it when it is solicited. Those who have
gifts of *prayer,* should not be backward to exercise
them for the edification of their brethren. Those
who have *penetration* and *sound judgment,* should
render their counsel and advice upon every occasion.
Persons of large and respectable *worldly connexions*
may often use their influence with great benefit to
the *temporal* affairs of the society.

And there is one line of charitable exertion, which
would be peculiarly beneficial, and which has been
too much neglected in all our societies; I mean the
practice of *respectable members reading the Scriptures
religious tracts, and sermons, in the habitations of the
poor.* I am aware that this is an age when many
run to and fro, and when lay preaching is carried
to a very improper and mischievous extent. Some
who have no other qualification for preaching than
boldness and ignorance, are every Sabbath employed, of whom it might be said, that it is a pity they
have not the gift of silence. Unfortunately, those
who are *most qualified,* are frequently *least disposed;*
while the least qualified, are the most zealous. But
how many wise, judicious, holy men, are there in
our churches, who would be most honourably and
most usefully employed, in reading the words of
life, and short evangelical sermons, in the cottages
of the poor! Let a convenient house be selected,
and the neighbours invited to attend: and who can
tell what vast benefit would accrue from such a
scheme? By the blessing of God upon these efforts,
reformation would be wrought in the lower classes; religion would gain an entrance where it could

9

be introduced by no other means, and our churches be replenished with holy, consistent members. Persons of *respectable circumstances in life*, especially, should thus employ themselves, as *their* situation gives them greater influence. Females may be thus engaged, without transgressing either against the injunction of the apostle, or the modesty which is so becoming their sex. I am astonished that means of usefulness so simple, so easy, and so efficient, are not more generally employed.

4. It is due to the authority of the church, that *every member should cordially submit to its discipline*. Without this, order would be destroyed, and the reign of anarchy introduced. This, indeed, as we have already considered, is essentially implied in the very act of joining the church; and no one ought to think of such an act of union, who is not determined to submit to its rules and its decisions.

CHAPTER VII.

THE DUTIES OF CHURCH MEMBERS TO THE MEMBERS OF OTHER CHRISTIAN SOCIETIES.

FIRST. In those cases where the churches are of a different denomination.

1. *We should respect their religious opinions and practices.*

They act conscientiously; and whatever is done at the dictate of conscience, is too sacred to be made the matter of ridicule. The way to bring the scorn of ungodly men upon *all* religion, is for religious people, differing upon minor points, to jest with each other's practices.

2. *Let us avoid religious bigotry and prejudice.*

By bigotry, I mean such an overweening attachment to our opinions and denomination, as alienates our affections from Christians of another name, and leads us to conclude there is little excellence or piety, except in our own communion.   Some Christians are so shortsighted by prejudice, that they cannot discern the most splendid exhibitions of moral excellence, if they are at the least removed from their own denomination.   The consideration, that a man is not of *their* party, is sufficient, in their evil eye, to dim the lustre of an example which angels admire, and to eclipse that living luminary, which, to the eye of Heaven, shines with most radiant glory. Their moral vision has so long and so intently pored over the minute distinctions of party, as to have acquired a contraction of power, which prevents them from comprehending and admiring, as they would otherwise do, the grander features of religion in general.

I know not a proof of true piety more decisive, and more pleasing, than that quick perception and fervent admiration of the beauties of holiness, which lead a man to recognise and love them, wherever they are seen, whether in his own denomination or in others.   " The evil to be deplored in the present state of the church, is the unnatural distance at which Christians stand from each other, the spirit of sects, the disposition to found their union on the wood, hay and stubble of human inventions, or disputable tenets, instead of the eternal Rock, the faith once delivered to the saints.   Surely, surely, we shall find a sufficient bond of union, a sufficient scope for all our sympathies, in the doctrine of the cross."*

---

* Robert Hall.

3. We should abstain from all officious contro-versy, or underhand proselytism.

I will not deny that there are occasions when our peculiar opinions may be brought forward with propriety and advocated with zeal; when silence would be lukewarmness, and not candour. But to be ever obtruding them upon the attention of others, and to be always seeking after opportunities of con-troversy, is as disgusting as it is pernicious; for while it offends others, it is sure to do harm to our own spirit.

Regarding the irreligious part of our population as an immense moral desert, surely there is scope enough for our zeal, to reclaim this immense waste, and convert it into the garden of the Lord, without employing our energies in altering the position of those plants and trees, which are already flourishing in the sacred enclosure. It is a far more honourable and useful kind of zeal, to convert sinners into Chris-tians, than real Christians of one name, into real Christians of another name.

SECONDLY. I shall now speak of the conduct of Christians to the members of other churches of their *own* denomination.

It does not unfrequently happen, that where two or more churches of the same denomination exist in a town, *a most unhappy, unscriptural, disgraceful temper is manifested towards each other.* All the feelings of envy, jealousy, and ill will, are cherished and displayed with as much, or more bitterness than two rival tradesmen would exhibit in the most de-termined opposition of interests. This is peculiarly the case *where two churches have been formed, by a schism, out of one.* Oftentimes the feud has been perpetuated through one generation, and has been bequeathed to the generation following. Can it be

that these are churches of saints? Can it be that
these are all one in Christ? Can it be that these
are societies, whose rule is the word of Christ, whose
conduct is the image of Christ, whose end is the
glory of Christ!!

Shame, public, deep, indelible shame on such societies! Is it thus that churches quarrel, to find
sport for their enemies? By all the regard which
is due to the authority of the Lord Jesus, by all the
constraining influence of his love, let such societies
be impelled to terminate their hateful strifes, which
are not more dishonourable to the cause of religion
in general, than they are injurious to the interests
of piety within their own immediate sphere of action. With what bitter taunts, with what sarcastic
triumph do profane and infidel spectators point to
such scenes, and ironically exclaim, " *See how these
Christians love one another!*"

Let us guard against this evil where it does *not*
exist, and endeavour to suppress it where it does.
Let us not look with envy and jealousy on the growing prosperity of other societies. Let us not consider *their* success as in any degree encroaching
upon *ours*. If we succeed more in *our own* church,
let us be thankful, but not boastful; if others take
precedence, let us be stirred up to affectionate, holy
emulation, but not to envy and jealousy.

A worthy minister, who used to preach a week
day lecture in the city of London, heard a friend
expressing his regret that it was so ill attended.
" Oh, that," replied the minister, " is of little consequence, as the gospel is preached by several others
in the same neighbourhood; and in such a situation,
for any one to be very desirous that people should
come and hear the gospel from *him*, instead of others,
seems as unreasonable, as it would be for one of the

shopmen in a large shop, to wish all the customers
to come to *his* particular part of the counter. If the
customers come at all, and the goods go off, in so
far as he feels an interest in the prosperity of the
shop, he will rejoice."   Beautiful and rare example
of true humility, pure zeal and genuine love to
Christ! Look at this, ye ministers and churches,
who quarrel with your neighbours, and scarcely speak
well of them, because they prosper no less than you!
Shall we feel mortified when immortal souls are saved,
because *we* are not the instruments of their conversion? Shall we say, if *we* cannot gather them into
our church, let them not be gathered? If two rival
physicians, who had each as much as he could do,
when the plague was raging in a town, looked with
envy and grudging on each other's success, what
should we say of *their* spirit? But such a temper
in these circumstances is far less criminal than the
envious disposition of some ministers and their
flocks.

There should be *a spirit of mutual affection* between the members of different churches. They
should love as brethren; and that this might not
be disturbed, they should avoid, when they meet in
their respective social circles, *all invidious and un-
charitable reference to the others.* Nothing is more
common than for the Christians of one society to
make the circumstances and faults of those of another the leading topics of conversation. Thus the
coals of strife are kindled in these *Christian* parties,
and every one present lends his breath to fan the
flame. It is melancholy indeed, when our houses
are thus converted into temples for the god of this
world, the divider of the brethren; and our family
altar is lent for an offering of scandal at his shrine.
Ministers, and leading persons in the company,

should always set their faces against this mischievous gossip. *All comparisons between the talents
of the ministers, and the respectability of their churches, should be carefully abstained from.* This is sure
to do harm. It is right for every church member
to be attached to his own pastor, and he may very
innocently think that his minister is the best preacher in the town; but it is insulting and mischievous
to express his opinion to those who prefer another.
It is not unusual for the pulpit to be converted into
a source of the most disgusting adulation, and for a
ministerial sycophant to flatter the pride of his flock,
by telling them how superior they are to all others
in affluence, liberality, and influence. Such fawning,
to say nothing of its littleness, is exceedingly injurious. What is intended as a compliment to one
church is felt as an insult by all others in its vicinity.
All boasting should be most conscientiously refrained
from, both on the part of ministers and people. If
they are in a state of spiritual prosperity, let them
be thankful, but not vain-glorious. " Charity vaunteth not itself, is not puffed up." The apostle delivered a very keen rebuke on those who are the
trumpeters of their own fame, when he said, " I
speak not after the Lord, but as it were foolishly in
the confidence of boasting. Seeing that many glory
after the flesh, I will glory also, for ye suffer fools
gladly."

*Church members should never resent by coldness,
and distance of behaviour, the conduct of those who
leave* THEIR *society, to join another in the same town.*
They have a right to exercise their own judgment
as well as we, and in their view, at least, have as
good reason for preferring the pastor to whom they
go, as we have for continuing with the one they
leave. They may separate too hastily, and not on

sufficient grounds; but that is their concern, not
ours, I have known cases in which both the minister and his flock have refused even the civilities
of ordinary intercourse to those who have left their
church to associate with another. This is a most
pitiful and unchristian disposition.

There are duties to be performed by the church
in its *collective* capacity towards other societies of
the same denomination.

1. *We should own them as churches of Christ,*
cherish the most friendly and fraternal feelings towards them, and hold Christian communion with
them in all the duties of our common faith and
practice,

Such appears to have been the feelings of the primary churches. "The churches of Christ salute
you." Rom. xvi. 16. "The church that is at Bab-
ylon, elected together with you, saluteth you." 1 Pet.
v. 13. "Ye are taught of God to love one another,
and ye do it towards all the brethren in Macedonia."
1 Thes. iv. 9, 10.

2. We should *receive their members when recom-
mended to us, and freely grant honourable recommendations of our members to them.*

"I commend unto you Phebe our sister, a servant
of the church at Cenchrea; receive her in the Lord
as becometh saints, and assist her in whatsoever
business she hath need of you." Rom. xvi. 1,
"They are the messengers of the churches; shew
ye to them, and before the churches, the proof of
your love." 2 Cor. viii. 23, 24,

3. We should *co-operate with neighbouring churches* for promoting the spread of the gospel, either by
local or general institutions.

Many objects of vast importance to the spread
of the gospe in the world can be accomplished by

the *union* of churches, which cannot be effected
without it.   Union is power.   Places of worship
may be opened, the faithful ministry of the word introduced, and churches planted in dark, benighted
villages; while all the grand and noble institutions
which are organized to save a perishing world, may
by this means receive additional support.   United
fires brighten each other's blaze, and increase each
other's intensity ; and thus the association of churches enkindles each other's zeal, and provokes one
another to love and good works.   Nor is *zeal* the
only Christian virtue promoted by such unions;
brotherly *love* is cherished and excited.   The presence of messengers from other churches at the annu-
al meetings of our societies, produces a friendly
feeling and brotherly interest, not unlike that which
a family experiences, when gathered together at
their Christmas party.   One great end of assembling
the males of the Jewish nation three times a year
before the ark, was to keep up a brotherly feeling
between the different and distant parts of the nation.
Nothing is so likely to cherish the fire of love, as
the fuel supplied by works of zeal.

4. We should be willing *to give and receive* AD-
VICE in cases of difficulty and importance.

Of course, the independence of the churches, and
the right of private judgment, should be vigilantly
watched, and sacredly preserved.   We have no dominion over each other's conduct, any more than
over each other's faith.   The idea of control is as
repugnant to revelation as it is to reason.   And we
are to resist unto blood, striving against the usurpa-
tion of foreign compulsory interference.   But *advice*
does not imply control.   The dread which has been
felt of the simple act of one church's asking the advice of a neighbouring minister, or an association

of ministers, in cases of extreme difficulty, discovers
a fear of domination, which is perfectly childish.
How consonant with all the dictates of reason, and
all the proceedings of civil life, is it, for two parties
in a state of litigation, to ask the opinion of a third;
or for one individual in difficulty, to solicit the advice of another.   When a minister and his flock are
in some critical situation, let them jointly agree to
lay their affairs before some two or three neighbouring ministers and laymen of sound judgment, for
counsel and direction; and how often, by this simple,
rational, scriptural process, would a society be
brought back from the brink of ruin to peace and
safety! But what if they should not take the advice
thus given?   They must then be left to themselves,
and would be but where they were before.   The
disposition which scorns to ask, and refuses to take
advice, savours far more of the pride of independence, than the love of peace; and of the temper
which courts interminable anarchy rather than be
indebted for the restoration of order, to the opinions
and persuasions of another.   Men which stand out
of the mist of passion, can see more than those enveloped in the fog.

5. We should take a *deep interest in the welfare
of other churches,* and in a suitable and proper manner express our sympathy, and afford to them our
assistance.

We should at our church meetings remember in
prayer, the cases of such as are in circumstances
of affliction; and in the event of the death of a pastor, how consoling would it be to a bereaved church,
to receive letters of condolence from neighbouring
societies!   There is one way, in which the most
effectual help may be rendered by one church to
another: I mean, *pecuniary assistance granted from*

such as are wealthy to those who are poor. We are informed, Acts xi. 29, 30, that the disciples at Antioch sent relief, according to their abilities, to the poor saints in Judea. "Concerning the collection for the saints, as I had given orders to the churches at Galatia: Even so do ye." 1 Cor. xvi. 1. I am aware, that this is sometimes done out of a fund, raised by the joint contributions of the churches in a county or district association; but how great would be the effect produced, if a church, in its individual capacity, were from year to year to send a donation to some poor community in its neighbourhood! What a lovely display of Christian feeling would this be! How would it endear the societies to each other! It would assist those to gain an efficient and settled minister, who, probably, but for such help, would only enjoy the precarious labours of occasional and incompetent preachers. The comfort of many faithful and laborious ministers would be thus promoted, and the kingdom of Jesus Christ enlarged.

Ye rich churches in our large cities, and in the country, who, without effort, can raise for your own pastors ample salaries, I appeal to your liberality, on behalf of those many churches scattered up and down the land, which are withering for the want of a little of that wealth, which you could spare, without lessening the comfort, either of your minister, or your families. I would not rob the funds of Missionary, or Bible Societies, to replenish the little store of gospel ministers at home; but I will say, that no foreign objects should be allowed to interfere with the claims of those deserving and holy men, who are labouring for souls amidst all the ills of poverty, and all the cares and woes which such ills must necessarily entail.

Where is the favoured individual, into whose lap
the bounty of Heaven has poured the abundance
of riches, and into whose heart divine grace has introduced the mercy that is full of good fruits?
here let him find an object worthy of his wealth
and of his zeal. Let him become the nursing father of our poor churches. *If he spend two thousand a year in this way, he may give forty pounds a
year to fifty ministers.* What a means of usefulness! How many infant churches would smile upon him from their cradle; and, as they turned upon
him their eyes glistening with gratitude, would exclaim, "My Father, my father!" In how many
church-books would his name be enrolled, amidst
the benedictions and prayers of the saints!

CHAPTER VIII.

THE DUTIES OF CHURCH MEMBERS IN THEIR PECU-
LIAR CHARACTER AND STATION.

I. THE pastor's wife.

A station so honourable, so important, so responsible, must necessarily be attended with duties numerous, difficult, and of great consequence. *As a
wife*, she should be a bright pattern of all that tender affection, that unsuspicious confidence, that
cheerful obedience, that undivided devotedness to
her husband's comfort, which such a relationship im-
plies; a lovely, spotless exhibition of connubial vir-

tue. No man is in greater need of all the force of conjugal sympathy and love, than a faithful minister.

As the female head of a family, she should direct her household affairs with judgment, and be a model of order, neatness, and domestic dicipline. A minister derives some degree of respectability from the state of his family. Home scenes, according as they are lovely or repulsive, form a beauteous halo round, or dark specks upon, the orb of his public character. It is required of him that he should rule well his own household; but in this he is *dependent upon his wife.* What a disgrace is it that *his* house should be such a scene of disorder, as to disgust, by its confusion, the more respectable part of his friends! Some people, if we were to judge from their habits, and their homes, seem to have been born *out of due time;* they look as if the era of their existence were the reign of chaos. Order is heaven's first law, and the laws of heaven certainly should govern the habitations of its ministers. If a *mother,* a minister's wife *should strive to excel in every maternal excellence.* How often is it the case, that a minister's children are talked of almost to a proverb, for their rudeness, ill behaviour, and wickedness; in such instances, much blame *must* be attached to the *mother.*

In her own *personal* character, there are two traits which should appear with peculiar prominence, and shine with attractive lustre in a minister's wife; these are PIETY and PRUDENCE. *Her* piety should not only be sincere, but *ardent;* not only unsuspected, but eminently conspicuous. Her habits, her conversation, her whole deportment, should bear the deep, bright impress of heaven. She should be the holiest, most spiritual woman in the church. Her *prudence* should equal her piety. Without the former, even the latter, however distinguished, would only half qualify her for her important station. Her prudence should display itself in all her conduct towards her *husband*. She should be very careful not to make him *dissatisfied with the situation he occupies.* Many a minister has been rendered uncomfortable in a situation of considerable usefulness, or has been led to quit it against the convictions of his judgment, by the capricious prejudices of his wife ; whose ambition has aspired to something higher, or whose love of change has coveted something new. A minister's wife should consult her husband's usefulness, and be willing to live in any situation, however self-denying its circumstances may prove, where this is promoted ; and considering the influence she has over his decisions, she should be very careful how she employs it *in those seasons when a change is meditated.* Her prudence should render her extremely careful, *not to prejudice her husband's mind against any individual who may have, designedly or unintentionally, injured her.* In not a few cases, have pastors been drawn into contention with some of their friends, by the imprudent conduct of their wives, who, possessing a morbid sensibility of offence, have reported, amidst much exaggeration, affronts which they ought not to have felt—or, feeling, ought to have concealed. Instead of acting as a *screen*, to prevent these petty vexations from reaching his ear, they have rendered their tongues a *conductor*, to convey them to his bosom. They should hide many things of this kind, which it is not important he should know, and soften others of which he cannot be ignorant.

In all cases *where her husband is the direct object of a supposed or real injury*, a minister's wife should be very cautious how she acts. Intended by nature, and inclined by affection, to be a partisan and an advocate in her husband's cause, so far as truth and holiness will allow, she should, at the same time, endeavour rather to *mitigate than exasperate* the displeasure of his mind. Her breath, in such cases, if imprudently employed, may fan a flame which, in its progress, may consume all the prosperity of the church, and half the reputation of her husband. Let her therefore *govern her own spirit*, as the best means of aiding to govern his. Let her calm, conciliate, and direct that mind, which may be too much enveloped in the mist of passion, to guide itself. Let her not go from house to house, dropping sparks and scintillations from a tongue set on fire of hell. If her husband be the head of a party, let her not envenom *their* minds with bitter words, which are sure to be rendered still more bitter, by the lying reporters who carry them to the opposite party. Prudence in a pastor's wife would have often saved a church from division.

A minister's wife *should never betray the confidence reposed in her by her husband, and report the opinions, views, and feelings, which he has communicated in the seasons of their private conversation.* The secrets he deposits in her bosom, are to be as sacredly preserved and guarded, as the ring, which, on the morning of their union, he placed upon her finger.

Prudence is to be displayed in all her conduct *towards the church.* Probably, the chief part of this virtue lies *in a proper government of the tongue.* A very large proportion of the disturbances which agitate the surface, and extend their influence to the very depths of society, arise from imprudent language. There appears to be, in one half of so-

ciety, an incurable propensity to relate what is to
the disadvantage of their neighbours; and in the
other half, an indestructible appetite to relish the
slander, when it is reported. Now a minister's
wife should most anxiously guard against this propensity in herself, and most assiduously labour to
abate this appetite in others. Let her, wherever
she goes, remember, that there are many waiting
and watching for her words, which they will be sure
to reverberate with the mimicry, though not with
the fidelity, of an echo. Let *her* tongue never deal
in sarcasm, satire, invective, censure, or slander.
Let it be an invariable rule with her, TO SPEAK ILL
OF NO ONE. *She should never appear fond of receiving ill reports from others.* If she have a taste
of this kind, gratification enough will be found her
Like a queen bee, she has no need to roam abroad
in quest of honey—she may sit at home in indolent repose, while the whole hive of gossips and tat-
tlers will collect for her an exuberant supply. Let
her rather discourage these humming, busy insects,
and convince them that she has neither ear for their
buzz, nor taste for their honey.

Let her never *betray a secret*, which she has been
compelled to receive ; nor *become umpire* between
two contending parties, since, in whatever way her
decision is pronounced, she is almost sure to offend
one of them. She should avoid, as much as possible,
the *appearance* of favouritism. Some there must
be, with whom she will be more intimate than others :
but this fact, if it be known, should be but little
seen ; and her friends should be always such, *as by
the common consent of the society would be allotted to
her ;* of course, they should not be minions selected
to sustain the character of fawning sycophants,
purveyors of news, or tools of selfishness. In all

her deportment towards the church, she should maintain a *dignified* consciousness of her station, blended with the greatest *affability* and *affection*. The law of kindness should be on her lips, and all her conduct should be so many displays of the meekness of wisdom. Her dignity should prevent the highest from being obtrusive, her kindness should make the lowest feel that she is accessible. Without being a busy body, and meddling with the concerns of others, she should *make the interests of her friends her own.* Her *advice* and assistance should always be granted when *asked,* but never distributed in a way that would render it unwelcome and little valued. Her influence should be discreetly exerted *in forming the general and pious habits of the younger females.* She should be the friend of the poor, and be often seen in the chambers of those of her own sex, when they are visited with sickness. With so much to engage her attention, she will have little leisure for *visits of useless show, or expensive intercourse.* Such she ought not to be expected to keep up, for her time can be more usefully and piously employed. For visits of mere gossip, or etiquette, she ought not to be put in requisition; and if she is, she should resist the attempt which is thus made to enslave her, by the bonds of fashion or of folly. She is the wife of a man, *whose master is God, whose business is the salvation of souls, whose scene of labour is the church of Christ, and the consequences of whose exertions, whether they succeed or fail, are infinite and eternal;* LET HER ACT ACCORDINGLY.

II. The deacons.

The institution of the deacon's office arose from a seemingly accidental circumstance which occurred in the church at Jerusalem, the particulars of which are recorded in the 6th chapter of the Acts of the Apostles.* The original design of this office, was to administer the bounty of the church. The first deacons were simply the *almoners* of their brethren. They dispensed the charities of the rich, for the relief of the poor. And *this*, whatever has been added by the usages of the churches, must *still* be considered as its *paramount duty*. What a lovely and attractive view does it give us of Christianity, and how strikingly characteristic of its merciful genius to behold it solemnly instituting an office, the chief design of which is, the comfort of its poorer followers! Where shall we find any thing analogous to this in other systems? Paganism and Mahometanism have nothing like it.

---

*Some persons are of opinion that this occurrence was not the origin of the deacon's office, and that the individuals there mentioned, are to be viewed, not as officers of the church, but merely as stewards of a public charity, who were appointed for a special occasion, and not as a general and authoritative precedent. It is said, in support of this opinion, that these individuals are not *called* deacons by the sacred historian, and that, in consequence, they cannot be proved to have been such. It is also contended, that St. Paul does not specify, in his epistle to Timothy, the duties of a deacon in such a way as to identify the office with what Luke, in the 6th of Acts, has stated to be the duties of the individuals there selected for the primitive church.

In reply to this, I contend that this *was* the origin of the deacon's office, and on the following grounds:

1st. Ecclesiastical history informs us, that the office was always considered, from the very earliest ages, as designed for the relief of the poor. If so, how natural is it to trace up its origin to the circumstance alluded to, which so easily accounts for it.

2nd. The solemnity with which the seven persons were set apart to their office, i. e. with prayer and imposition of hands, looks as if their appointment was to be considered as a standing and authoritative precedent.

By a reference to the origin of the office, we shall learn how widely some religious communities have departed from the design of this simple, merciful, and useful institution. "Those who perverted all church orders," says Dr. Owen, "took out of the hands and care of the deacons, that work which was committed to them by the Holy Ghost in the apostles, and for which end alone their office was instituted in the church, and assigned other work unto them, whereunto they were not called and appointed. And whereas, when all things were swelling with pride and ambition in the church, no sort of its officers contenting themselves with their primitive institution, but striving by various degrees to be somewhat, in name and thing, that was high and aloft,

---

3d. If this be not the origin of the deacon's office, where shall we find the account? and what is still stronger, if this be not the institution, St. Paul has given directions about an office, the duties of which are, in that case, not mentioned in the Word of God. He has certainly said nothing himself of its design—a circumstance which is strongly presumptive of the truth of my view of the case, since his silence seems to imply that the duties of the deacon were already too well known to need that he should specify them. His very omission is grounded on some previous institution. Where shall we find this, but in Acts vi.?

4th. The *reason* of the appointment in question, is of *permanent* force, i. e. that those who minister in the Word, should not have their attention diverted by temporal concerns; and, therefore, seems as if a *permanent office* was then established.

5th. I would ask any one who takes a different view from that which I hold, what are the duties of the deacons mentioned by Paul? If he reply, as I think he must, "To attend to the concerns of the poor," I would still inquire how he knows that. If he answer, The testimony of ecclesiastical history—I would still ask, On what the immemorial usage of the church could be founded, if not on the fact mentioned by Luke in the Acts of the Apostles?

there arose from the name of this office the *meteor* of an *arch deacon*, with strange power and authority never heard of in the church for many ages. But this belongs to the mystery of iniquity, whereunto neither the Scripture nor the practice of the primitive churches, do give the least countenance. But some think it not inconvenient to *sport themselves* in matters of church order and constitutions."*

The church of England, which retains some of the corruptions of the church of Rome, has imitated her in the total alteration of this office. In that communion, the deacon is not a secular, but a spiritual officer, and his post is considered as the first grade in the ascent to the episcopal throne. He is a preacher, and may baptize, but not administer the eucharist. He is, in fact, half priest, half layman, and does not altogether put off the laic, nor put on the cleric character, till his second ordination to the full orders of the priesthood. The church-warden and the overseer share between them the office of the deacon.

Abuses of this office, however, are not confined to the churches of Rome and of England, but may be found in the ecclesiastical polity of those who separate from both. What is the deacon of some of our independent communities? Not simply the laborious, indefatigable, tender-hearted dispenser of the bounty of the church, the inspector of the poor, the comforter of the distressed; no, but "the bible of the minister, the patron of the living, and the wolf of the flock;" an individual, who, thrusting himself into the seat of government, attempts to lord it over God's heritage, by dictating alike to the pastor and the members; who thinks that, in virtue of his

---

* Dr. Owen on Church Government, &c. 131.

office, his opinion is to be law in all matters of church government, whether temporal or spiritual. This man is almost as distant from the deacon of apostolic times, as the deacon of the Vatican. Such men there have been, whose spirit of domination in the church has produced a kind of *diaconophobia* in the minds of many ministers.*

I do beseech those who bear this office to look to its origin, and learn that it is an office of *service*, which gives no authority, or power, or rule in the church, beyond the special work for which it is appointed, and that is, *to provide for the comfort of the poorer brethren*. This is their business. It is true, that by the usages of our churches, many things have been added to the duties of the office, beyond its original design; but this is mere matter of expediency.

It is often said that the duty of the office is to serve tables; the table of the Lord, the table of the minister, and the table of the poor. If it be meant that this was the *design* of its appointment, I deny the statement, and affirm that the table of the poor, is the deacon's appropriate and exclusive duty. Whatever is conjoined with this, is *extra diaconal* service, and vested in the individual, merely for the sake of utility. Such increase of their duties, I admit, is wise and proper. We need persons to take care of the comfort of the minister—to provide for the holy feast of the Lord's supper—to direct the arrangements of all matters connected with public worship; and who so proper for this, as the breth-

---

* The author writes from observation, not from experience; besides the eight deacons with whom he acts at present, he has already outlived eight more, and both the dead and the living have been his comfort and joy.

ren who already fill an office, of which temporalities are the object and design? But these are all *additions* to the paramount duty of the deacon, which is to *take care of the poor.*

Let it not be thought, that this is exhibiting the office in a naked, and meagre, and degrading point of view; or as shorn of the beams of its brightest glory. What can be a more happy or more honourable employment, that to distribute the alms of the brethren, and visit the habitations of the poor, like angels of mercy, with words of peace upon their lips, and the means of comfort in their hands? A faithful, laborious, affectionate deacon, must necessarily become the object of justly deserved regard in the church, and be looked up to with the esteem and veneration, which are paid by a grateful dependent family to their sire. The poor will tell him their wants and woes, spiritual and temporal; and ask his advice with implicit confidence. He will move through the orbit of his duty amidst the prayers and praises of his brethren, and in measure may adopt the language of Job—"When the ear heard me, then it blessed me; and when the eye saw me, then it gave witness to me; because I delivered the poor that cried, and the fatherless, and him that had none to help him. The blessing of him that was ready to perish came upon me, and I caused the widow's heart to sing for joy. I was eyes to the blind, and feet was I to the lame. I was *a father to the poor,* and the cause which I knew not, I searched out." Surely, surely, here is honour, much pure, legitimate, exalted honour. Such a man *must* be, and *ought* to be a person of influence in the society; but it is the influence of *character,* of *goodness,* of *usefulness.* Let him have his periodical visitations of the poor. Let him go and see their wants and woes in their *own* habitations, as well as bid them come and tell their sorrows in *his*. Let him be full of compassion and tender hearted; let his eyes drop pity, while his hands dispense bounty; let him be affable and kind as well as attentive. And such a man shall want neither honour nor power amongst his brethren, although, at the same time, he be peaceful as a dove, meek as a lamb, and gentle as a little child.

The apostle is very explicit in his statement of the *qualifications* which the deacons should possess. "Likewise must the deacons be grave," *i. e.* men of serious and dignified deportment; "not double tongued," *i. e.* sincere, not addicted to duplicity of speech; "not given to much wine; not greedy of filthy lucre; holding the mystery of the faith in a pure conscience," *i. e.* attached to the doctrines of the gospel, and exhibiting their holy influence in a spotless life; "and let them also first be proved; then let them use the office of a deacon, being found blameless. Let them be the husband of one wife, ruling their children and their own houses well." 1 Tim. iii. 8—13.*

Deacons should remember, that *all* these qualifications should be found embodied, as much as possible,

---

* The allusion made to the deacons' wives, appears to me to be a mistranslation, and in the original refers to a class of female office bearers in the primitive church. "*Even so the women.*" As the manners of the Greeks and Romans, and especially of the Asiatics, did not permit men to have much intercourse with women of character, unless they were relations, it was proper that an order of female assistants should be instituted for visiting and privately instructing the young of their own sex, and for catechising females of any age. And as the church was then much persecuted, and many of its members were often condemned to languish in a prison, these holy women were, no doubt, peculiarly useful in visiting the captive Christians,

in *each individual,* holding the office ; and not merely some in one and some in another, till the character is formed by the joint number, but not in each
member of the deaconry.   Some have contended for
plurality of elders in a church, because it is impossible to find all the qualifications of a Christian bishop stated by the apostle, in *one* person.   We are
to look for one excellence in one man, and another
in the second, and what is wanting in one will be
made up in another, until their defects and attainments are made to unite, like the corresponding
parts of a dovetail joint.   I confess, however, that
this way of making church officers, as it were by
patch work, appears to me a most absurd idea.

The deacons, from their being officers in the
church, although their office refers to temporalities,
and also from their being generally acquainted with
the affairs of the church, will be considered by every
wise and prudent minister, as his privy council in
his spiritual government, and should be always
ready to afford him their advice in a *respectful* and
unobtrusive manner.   " Christian brethren," said
a preacher on this subject, " give to the minister I love, for a deacon, a man in whose house he
may sit down at ease, when he is weary and loaded

---

and performing for them many kind offices which *their* sex can
best render.   Such an one, in all probability, was Phebe, mentioned Rom. xvi. 1.   Such were the widows spoken of 1 Tim.
v.   Such were Euodia and Syntyche, Phil. iv. 3.   Clement of
Alexandria reckons *widows* amongst ecclesiastical persons.
" There are many precepts in Scripture for those who are chos-
en, some for priests, others for bishops, others for deacons,
others for widows."   Pliny, in his celebrated Epistle to Trajan,
is thought to refer to deaconesses, when, speaking of two female Christians whom he put to the torture, he says, " quæ
ministræ dicebantur ;" i. e. who were called deaconesses.

with care; into whose bosom he may freely pour his sorrows, and by whose lips he may be soothed when he is vexed and perplexed; by whose illuminated mind he may be guided in difficulty; and by whose liberality and cordial co-operation, he may be animated and assisted in every generous undertaking." And I would add, who would do all this in the spirit of humble, modest, and unauthoritative affection.

In the transactions of church business, the deacons should exert no other influence than that which arises from the esteem and affection in which they are held by the people. All personal and official authority should be abstained from. Their opinion should ever be stated with pre-eminent modesty; for if it be a wise one, its wisdom will commend itself to the judgment of the people, whose hearts are already prepared by affection and esteem to yield to its influence. Whereas, the wisest opinion, if delivered dogmatically, will often be resisted, merely because it is attempted to be *imposed*.

If a man deserve influence, he will be sure to have it without seeking it, or designedly exerting it; if he do not deserve it, and still seek it, he is sure to be resisted.

"The deacon's duty to the people, is to promote, so far as he is able, the happiness of individuals, and the welfare of the society. In his intercourse with them, he should be firm and unbending in principle, but kind and conciliatory in temper and in manner. In those parts of his office, which are sometimes very irksome and arduous, from the difficulty of serving all according to their wishes, he should guard against every thing which even appears to be harsh and unkind. More especially should he do this, when he finds it impossible, in consistency with his duty to others, to fulfil their desires. The apparently insig-

11

nificant circumstance, which will often occur in our congregations, of being unable to accommodate an individual, or a family, with a seat, may be mentioned with so much kindness, and with such unfeigned regret that it is so, as to lead the individual, or the family, patiently to wait for a more favourable opportunity ; or it may be done, although without design, in a tone of so much indifference, as to lead the disappointed applicant to relinquish the hope of success, and to leave the place.   The secret charm by which the deacon's office may be rendered comfortable to himself, and beneficial to others, is that golden precept of inspiration, " Let all your things be done with charity ;" or, as Dr. Doddridge better translates the passage, " Let all your affairs be transacted in love."   1 Cor. xvi. 14.

III. Heads of families.

The station occupied by such persons, is exceedingly important, and therefore very responsible. We naturally look to the families of professing Christians for the materials with which the " spiritual house" is to be repaired amidst the spoliations of sin and death.   A large proportion of our members are the children of the righteous, and our churches would be still more enriched with the fruits of domestic piety, if that piety itself were more ardent and more exemplary.   It is impossible to urge in terms too strong, the sacred duties of Christian masters, mistresses, and parents.   *Their* influence on the prosperity of the church is greater than is generally conceived, or can be fully stated.   The duties of such persons are of a two-fold nature.

1. The primary ones, of course, relate to your CHILDREN.   It is the command of God to train them up in the fear, and nurture, and admonition of the Lord.   Let your first, and deepest, and most lasting

solicitude be for the formation of their *religious* character, and the *salvation of their souls.* Let this regulate all your conduct towards them. Let it impel
you to adopt a system of instruction and discipline,
which shall have a close and constant bearing on
their moral and religious habits. Let it guide you
in the choice of *schools* where they are to be educat-
ed, the families into which they are to be appren-
ticed. Act so, as that they may clearly discern,
that your most ardent prayer, your most anxious
concern, is, that they may be *truly pious.* They
should see this interwoven with all your conduct towards them; and behold a uniform, consistent, constant effort to accomplish this object. Let them
hear it expressed in your advice and prayers, and
see it manifested in all your arrangements. Alas!
alas! how many children of church members are
there, who, if they were asked the question, " What
is your father and mother's chief concern for you ?"
would be obliged to reply, " That I might excel in
fashionable accomplishments, and make a figure in
the drawing room." There appears to me to be, at
the present moment, a most criminal neglect, on the
part of Christian parents, of the RELIGIOUS education
of their children. Every thing is sacrificed to the
lighter and more frivolous accomplishments of the
female character, and to the literary and scientific
acquisitions of boys. *Religion is a secondary matter.* But ought it to be so ? Ought it not rather
to be the *one thing needful* for our children, as well
as for ourselves ?

That Christian who would carry on a system of
religious education with success, should enforce it
with all the commanding influence of a HOLY EXAM-
PLE. Let your children see all the " beauties of
holiness," reflected from your character, and the

grand outline of Christian *morality* filled up with all
the delicate touches and varied colouring of the
Christian *temper*. The heathens had their **Penates,**
or little shrines of their gods, which they kept in
their own habitation, to remind them of the objects
of their religious veneration and trust. Be you to
your families instead of these household gods, by
being lovely images of the great Jehovah. Let
your children have this conviction in their hearts,
" If there be but two real Christians in the world,
my father is one, and my mother is the other." It
is dreadful, but not uncommon for children to employ themselves in contrasting the appearance
which their parents make at the Lord's table and at
their own; in the house of God, and at home.

FAMILY PRAYER should be performed with great
punctuality, constancy and *seriousness*. It is of
course presumed that every Christian does pray
with his household. It should not be performed so
late in the evening that the family are more fit for
sleep than devotion, nor so late in the morning, as
for business to interrupt it. It should ever be conducted with the most solemn devotion, and never
rendered tedious by *extreme length*. It should be
very simple, and have *special* reference to the case
of the *children* and the *servants*. That it might be
performed with regularity, heads of families should
rarely *sup from home*. It is a disgrace for a Christian master or parent to be often seen in the streets
at eleven o'clock at night.

Professing Christians should resist the entrance
of *worldly conformity* into their families. Expensive
entertainments, gay parties, vain and frivolous
amusements, showy modes of dress, should be most
cautiously avoided. Religion will not dwell amidst
such scenes; her refined and spiritual taste is soon

offended, and she retires. A Christian's habits should be simple and spiritual. If it be his aim to approach as nearly as possible to the manners of the world without actually being numbered with its votaries, his children will be restrained with difficulty on the right side of the line of demarcation, and be perpetually longing and trying to push onward. The miserable efforts, made by some professing Christians, to be thought people of *taste* and *fashion;* to live half way between the tradesman and the gentleman, show how ill they bear the Christian yoke, and how nearly they are resolved to cast it away as an encumbrance. We should despise these things wherever we see them, if they did not prefer claims upon our *pity*, still stronger than those upon our *scorn*. When a worldly temper has crept into the circle of a Christian church, piety retires before it, and the spirit of error soon enters to take possession of the desolate heritage.

2. There is another duty which devolves on those whom Providence has placed at the head of a family, and that relates to their DOMESTICS.

Heads of families should manifest a kind solicitude for the temporal comfort of their domestics, and especially a deep solicitude for their *spiritual welfare.* They should take care that they are provided with Bibles, and furnished with a few religious books to peruse on the Sabbath, and at other intervals of leisure. In every respectable habitation, there should certainly be a *kitchen library*, comprising a few plain, interesting, moral, and religious treatises. Great care should be taken, in the arrangement of domestic affairs, to afford opportunities to their households, to attend the solemnities of *public worship*. It is too common to allow them this privilege only in the afternoon, which is a part of the

day least favourable to religious instruction and im
pression. Is not this a most cruel deprivation? If
the heads of a family find the afternoon a dull and
profitless season, how much more so must it be to
them, who, to the labour of the week, have added
that of the Sabbath morning!

And why cannot the domestics be permitted to
go to worship on the Sabbath *morning?*—O! tell
it not in Gath—because they are kept at home *to
cook a dinner for the parlour.* Shame and disgrace
on that professing Christian, who will not forego
the gratifications of his palate, though it be to aid
in the salvation of souls. How can he enjoy the
roasted joint, when he remembers that one of the
family has been, at his command, devoting the Lord's
day to prepare the feast? *He* comes from the
house of God, perhaps from the sacramental table,
and, in the hearing of his domestics, talks of the
precious season he has experienced ; while *they* re-
vile, as mere disgusting cant, the religious conversation of a man who would rob the souls of others to
pamper his appetite. Such men are worse than Esau ;
he sold his own birthright for the gratification of his
palate, but they sell the birthright of others. Yes, the
Sabbath is their *birthright*, or rather is granted to them
by *charter* from God ; and no man can alienate the sacred gift from them, without committing a felony of the
worst kind. Is it not enough, that they labour for our
comfort *six* days in the week, but they must also have
the *seventh*, the season of repose, taken from them.

Great, very great reproach is frequently brought
upon religion by the manner in which many professors conduct themselves towards those, who have
·claims upon them for something more than their
wages. It has been said that no man is great in
the eyes of his valet. I am afraid that the senti-

ment admits of extension, and that it might be said, that few men are *exemplary* for piety in the eyes of their servants.

IV. Domestics.

There is no class of church members, for whom I feel more anxious, than for domestics. Cut off, in a considerable degree, by their very situation, from *pastoral attentions;* urged forward in a course of labour, which in many cases has no intervals of rest; often most cruelly deprived of the repose of the Sabbath; it is difficult, indeed, for them to keep up the power, or enjoy the consolations of personal religion. *They* have peculiar need to watch, lest the flame of piety should languish and expire in their hearts.

It is quite interesting to observe how particular the apostle is in his direction to servants. " Servants, be obedient to them that are your masters according to the flesh, with fear and trembling, in singleness of your heart as unto Christ; not with eye service, as men pleasers, but as the servants of Christ, doing the will of God from the heart; with good will doing service as to the Lord, and not to men." Eph. vi. 5—7. The same sentiments are repeated, Col. iii. 22—25. Titus ii. 9, 10. It is to such that the solemn and striking admonition is addressed, "to *adorn* the doctrine of God our Saviour in all things." Even the sublime doctrine of a redeeming God, that bright effulgence which has issued from the fountain of light, is susceptible of decoration, and receives its adorning from the consistent conduct, not merely of a religious monarch, philosopher, or scholar, but of a Christian *servant.* The most scrupulous honesty, the most unwearied diligence, the most humble submission, the most inviolable truth, are necessary to this. Servants should

make *the interests of the family their own,* and act in
all things towards their employer's property as if
they were its *possessors.* The apostle has laid uncommon stress upon servants' being uniformly *the
same* for fidelity, and honesty, and diligence, whether
in the *presence* or *absence* of their employers. All
they do, even the most ordinary duties of their station, is to be done as to *the Lord,* and he is every
where present. Their religion should be distinctly
seen in the manner of performing the *duties of their
station;* and it should be obvious that their piety has
improved them as servants.

Where they are placed in *irreligious families,*
"let them count their own masters worthy of all
honour, that the name of God and his doctrine be
not blasphemed." 1 Tim. vi. 1. Let them not feel
at liberty to treat their employers with contempt
and neglect, as mere *carnal* persons; for religion
does not abolish the distinctions of society, nor the
rights connected with them. I scarcely know one
character in the private walks of life, that has a
fairer opportunity to glorify God, than a *religious
servant* in an ungodly family. It will be a fine testimony to the excellence of piety, when we shall
hear even *irreligious* persons generally say, "We
will never have, if we can help it, any but *religious*
servants, for we have seen that piety renders them
faithful, humble, diligent and trust-worthy."

Where pious servants are placed in irreligious
families, they should certainly endeavour to act the
part of reformers; but it must be rather by their
actions than their words. Mr. Jay informs us, that
in his conversation with a pious domestic, she ex-
claimed, "My master and mistress will not hear a
word I have to say on religion." "What *you* SAY,"
he replied; "*you* should *do,* and not say. You should

instruct them by early rising, by diligence, by fidelity, by not replying again." Servants have a most
favourable opportunity of letting their employers *see*
what religion is: but then it is not merely by going
to meeting or church, but by diligence, good temper, order and fidelity, obliging conduct, submission,
meekness, and letting it be apparent that all this
is the result of their religion.

"They that have *believing* masters, let them not
despise them because they are brethren, but rather
do them service because they are faithful and beloved, partakers of the benefit." 1 Tim. vi. 2.
They are not in such circumstances to abate one
iota of that reverence and obedience which are
due to them: for though by the law of Christ they
are brethren, this does not destroy their superiority.
It is no uncommon thing for religious servants *to
manifest such a degree of consequence,* and *to expect so
much deference,* as to lead some heads of families to
say that they would rather have merely good *moral*
servants, than *religious* ones. In some cases, where
they have been deprived, not by any capricious or
arbitrary arrangement, but the unavoidable necessities of the family, from enjoying so many opportunities as they could wish; when they have been un-
expectedly deprived of the privilege of attending
public worship, perhaps only for a *single season,* they
have manifested so much petulance, and entered upon their home duties with so much sullen reluctance
and ill humour, that their religion, or rather, I ought
to say, their *want* of it, has become a source of disgust and uneasiness. The means of grace ought
to be valued and improved; but the *occasional* and
unavoidable loss of them should not be attended with
the destruction of the Christian temper

It would be well, on entering upon a place, to

have an understanding with employers, on the sub ject of attendance at public worship. This would prevent all disagreement afterwards, or would at least furnish a compact to which reference might be made in future. It cannot surely be necessary to admonish such as make a profession of religion, never to go into any situation, whatever pecuniary advantages may present themselves, in which they are prevented from attending the public means of grace. That person cannot really seek *first* the kingdom of God, who, for the sake of higher wages, would go into a place, which excludes all enjoyment of the Sabbath, and the house of God, and almost all opportunities of *private prayer*. Those who have obtained comfortable situations, should be anxious to *retain them ;* for it is not creditable to their profession, to be often *changing places.* It would also be honourable to their characters, to be ever distinguished· for neatness, rather than *gaudiness* of attire. A love for dress is censurable in *all* professing Christians, but most of all, in those whose means scarcely enable them to command the vanities of this world. How much more would it be to their honour and comfort, *to lay by a portion of their wages for a time of need!*

V. Young persons.

These generally form a very considerable class of our members, and have duties to perform appropriate to their age and station. They should be very watchful against the sins to which the ardour and inexperience of their years may expose them. They should flee *youthful lusts*, and be very cautious to abstain from *vanity* and *self-conceit.* Their introduction at so early a period to the church, is very apt, in some cases, to inflate them with pride, to invest them with self-importance, and impair that

modesty of deportment, which is the loveliest orna-
ment of their character.   In all their conduct
towards the church, there should be an amiable *re-
tiredness* of disposition.   They should be *seen* at
the church meetings, but very rarely *heard*.   It is
difficult to conceive of a more disgusting or mischievous spectacle, than a young member *dogmatically* stating his opinion, and *pertinaciously* enforcing it, before men who were grey in the service
of God before his head was covered with the down
of infancy.

Young Christians should be very careful not to
form *matrimonial connexions*, in opposition to the
apostolic injunction, "not to be unequally yoked
together with unbelievers."   Both reason and revelation unite their testimony against the practice of
· Christians marrying *irreligious* persons.   What an
interruption to conjugal comfort, what an obstacle
to domestic piety, what an injury to the cause of
religion, does such a practice bring with it!

There is one way, in which young Christians
may bring great reproach upon the cause of God,
and that is by engaging the affections of a female,
and then abandoning her.   This is a species of cruelty which certainly deserves, and always receives,
the severest reprobation.   It is dishonourable in a
man of the world, much more in a church member.

VI.   Rich members.

It is true our churches do not *abound* with such
persons; but, enriched as our cause is with the principles of divine truth, and patronised by the smiles
of Heaven, we can dispense with the blazonry and
patronage of secular distinctions.

There are men, however, who, amidst the accu-
mulations of increasing wealth, remain firmly attached to the principles of the gospel, and who delight

to lavish their fortunes in supporting the cause they love and espouse. Let them consider it as their incumbent duty, to consecrate no small portion of their affluence, not merely in propagating the prin-ciples of Christianity abroad, but upholding *the cause of truth* at home. The erection of chapels, the sup-port of seminaries, the maintenance of poor minis ters, the establishment of churches, should with them be objects of deep anxiety.

Let them, in order to abound more and more in such efforts, as well as to exhibit a bright example of pure and undefiled religion, avoid all *unnecessary worldly conformity, and all expensive modes of living.* Something is due to their rank and station, but more than is *necessary*, ought not to be conceded. There is, in the present age, a disposition, even in profess-ing Christians, to a showy and expensive style of liv-ing, which cannot be more effectually repressed, than by the plain and simple habits of those who are known to have an easy access to all the elegances and splendours of life. "Charge them that are rich in this world, that they be not high-minded, nor trust in uncertain riches, but in the living God, who giveth us all things richly to enjoy ; that they do good, that they be rich in good works, ready to distribute, will-ing to communicate." Such was the admonition of St. Paul to Timothy, from which we gather, that rich Christians ought to be far more anxious to lay *out* that to lay *up* their fortunes. When we enter their mansions and see magnificence in every room, luxu-ry on every table ; when we see their gay equipage, we cannot help saying, "How much ought a disciple of Jesus, who lives in this manner, to give away to the cause of religion and humanity, before he is justified in such an expenditure." There appears to me to be yet wanting a *proportionate* liberality on the part of the *rich*. *Their* efforts bear no comparison with those of the middling classes, and of the poor. The former give of their abundance, the latter of their little ; at most, the former only tax their *luxuries*, but the latter, their *comforts* and *necessaries*.

Rich Christians should be exceedingly attentive to the *wants* and *comforts* of their *poorer brethren*. There is a great lack of this in the churches of Christ. " Whoso hath this world's goods, and seeth his brother have need, and shutteth up his bowels of compassion from him, how dwelleth the love of God in him ?" 1 John iii. 7. Such persons should carefully and tenderly inquire into the condition of the poor, and not content themselves with a monthly contribution at the Lord's supper, to be disposed of by the deacons. And it would be well if the deacons were often to go to the habitations of the more affluent members of the church, and lay before them the case of their destitute brethren.

The more wealthy members should be **very** cautious *not to assume undue power in the government of the church*. The distinctions of wealth have no place in the kingdom of Christ. No haughty airs, no proud scorn of the opinions of others less affluent than themselves, no overbearing urgency in stating their own views, should ever be discovered in their conduct in the transactions of church business. Their superior wealth, if not attended with a spirit of domination, is sure in every case to procure for them all the deference that is compatible with the independence of the church.

In short, the vices to which the rich are more particularly exposed, and against which they should vigilantly guard, are pride, haughtiness, love of money, idleness, self-indulgence, luxury, **worldly** conformity, ecclesiastical domination, and oppression of the poor. The virtues they are called to exercise are gratitude to God, humility and condescension to men, economy, temperance and liberality, together with tender sympathy to their poorer brethren, and a generous regard to the support of the cause of pure religion and general benevolence.

VII. The poor.

Contentment with such things as they have, and an *unmurmuring submission* to the appointment of Providence, are most obviously *their* duty, and should be conspicuously manifested in all their deportment. It should not appear as if they thought it hard, that their lot was cast in the humble vale of poverty. A cheerful resignation to the irremediable ills of their station, a frame of mind that looks as if they were so grateful for the blessings of grace, as to be almost insensible to the privations of poverty, is one of the ways in which poor Christians may signally glorify God.

The poor should watch against an *envious* spirit. "Grudge not one against another," said the apostle. They should be conspicuous for their *industry*, nor wish to eat the bread of idleness. "For this is commanded you, that if any would not work, neither should he eat. For some walk among you disorderly, working not at all, but are busy bodies. Such we command and exhort by the Lord Jesus Christ, that with quietness they work and eat their own bread." 2 Thess. iii. 10—12. The poor have no right, therefore, to expect, that in consequence of their association with a Christian church, they are in any measure released from the obligation of the most unwearied industry. They are not to be supported by the society in idleness, nor ought they to look for any pecuniary allowance while *able to provide for themselves and their family.* The religion of Jesus Christ was never intended to establish a system of *religious pauperism.* It is to be feared, that not a few have entered into Christian fellowship on purpose to *share its funds.* This is an awful case, wherever it occurs, and should make all the poor members of our churches tremble at the most distant approximation to such a crime.

The only times in which members should feel that they have claims upon the funds collected at the Lord's supper, are, when *sickness* has entered their dwelling, when age has *incapacitated* them for labour, or when the produce of their industry is too scanty to procure the necessary comforts of life.*

The poor should not be *exorbitant* in their expectations of relief; and should the bounty of the church flow less freely towards them than they have reason and right to look for, they should not indulge in the language of reproach and complaint. Not that they are forbidden in mild and modest language to represent their situation to the deacons.

They should be particularly careful not to mani-

---

* It is a question that has been sometimes agitated, whether it is right for a church to allow the members to apply for assistance from the town. Such a question, however, may be set at rest by a law, which, where it really exists, allows of no farther appeal; I mean the law of *necessity.* Some churches are composed in a great measure of poor persons, and even of the remainder who are not poor, there are few above the rank of small tradesmen. In this case, when trade is bad, and disease is prevalent it is next to impossible, if not quite so, for the church to relieve all the wants of its members. But setting aside this extreme case, what law is violated, what obligation is broken through, by our members' applying for a portion of that property, which is collected for them no less than others, and to which they are legally entitled in common with others? There can be nothing wrong on the part of the poor themselves in applying for this relief, unless they are so well provided for by

fest an *encroaching* and begging disposition. I
have known cases, in which the greatest disgust
and the most unconquerable prejudice have been
excited against individuals, by their proneness to
beg of every one that visited them, till at length
their fellow-members, wearied *too soon*, it must be
admitted, with the language of perpetual complaint
and petition, have left off to visit them altogether.

Cleanliness is a very incumbent duty of the poor.
Their cottages may be lowly, but certainly need not
be dirty. Filthiness is one species of vice, and
cleanliness is not only *next* to godliness, but a *part*
of it. The credit of religion often depends on *little*
things, and this is one of them.

VIII. Tradesmen.

A very large number of our church members are
engaged in the pursuits of trade, manufacture, or
commerce ; and from their very calling are exposed
to peculiar dangers, which must be met with proportionate vigilance.

It is highly incumbent upon them to take care
against a *worldly spirit*. They are in extreme peril

the church as not to need it. In this case their application
would be manifestly an imposition. The only question is,
whether a church, tolerably favoured with affluent members,
ought to allow such application. It would certainly be an act
of great generosity in such a church, to render their members
independent of assistance from the town · but I do not see by
what law this is actually their duty. We stand in a double relationship to the poor, as fellow-citizens and fellow Christians ;
in our former connexion we may ask for them a share of a
civil fund, while in the latter we relieve them from a still more
sacred source. The poor by entering our churches do not for-
feit any of their *civil* rights, and since they are legally entitled
to the assistance of their fellow-subjects, it is not necessary
that we should take upon ourselves, as *Christians*, those burdens which others are bound to sustain as *citizens*.

of losing the power of godliness from their hearts, and joining the number of those, of whom it is said, in the expressive language of St. Paul, that "they mind earthly things." Such persons look upon the possession of wealth as "the one thing needful." It is their chief object of pursuit, the chief source of happiness. Nothing modifies or mitigates the desire of riches. They are of the earth, earthy. Now certainly a Christian tradesman is, or ought to be, of another spirit than this. He should be industrious, frugal, and persevering in his attention to the concerns of this world; but still there should be in his mind an ultimate and supreme regard to the possession of everlasting life. He ought not to be slothful in business, but then he *must* be fervent in spirit, serving the Lord. He should be seen to unite the *clever tradesman* and *sincere Christian;* and to be *busy* for *both* worlds. The men of this world should be constrained to say of him, " This man is as attentive to business, and as clever in it as we are; but we can perceive in all he does, an inflexible regard to principle, an invariable reference to religion. We can discover no lack of diligence or prudence ; but it is perfectly evident, that his heart and highest hope are in heaven. He is neither so elated in prosperity, nor so depressed in adversity, as we are. He has some secret source of happiness, of which we are not possessed; and his eye is upon some standard of action, which we do not recognise. He is a *Christian* as well as a *tradesman.*"

What a testimony ! Who can obtain a higher one ? Who should seek less ?

There are many snares to which a Christian tradesman is peculiarly exposed in the *present* mode of conducting business. The stream of trade no longer glides along its old accustomed channel, where established and ordinary causes impelled its motions and guided its course; but under the violent operation of new and powerful impulses, it has of late years started from its course, and, with the rapidity of a torrent or the force of an inundation, has swept away the restraint of religious principle, and carried a deluge of dishonesty over the moral world.

It is quite time for Christian tradesmen to return, in their mode of conducting business, to the sound principles of Christian morality. Let them beware of *excessive speculation;* and where the property with which they trade, is scarcely their own, let them err rather on the side of caution than of enterprise. Let them beware of all dishonourable means of propping up a sinking credit. Let them view with abhorrence those practices which are resorted to only by rogues and swindlers. Let them tremble and blush at a single effort to extricate themselves from difficulty, which the world would condemn as unfair or dishonourable. Let their motto be, " whatsoever things are true, whatsoever things are honest, whatsoever things are just, whatsoever things are pure, whatsoever things are lovely, whatsoever things are of good report, if there be any virtue, and if there be any praise, think on these things."*   Phil. iv. 7.

A Christian should be careful not to conceal, *too long,* the fact of his being in a state of *insolvency.* A false pride, or a foolish hope, has led many to the dishonour of their profession, to go on floundering in difficulties, while every struggle has only carried them farther and farther into the current of

---

* See Dr. Chalmer's admirable sermons on the moral principles of trade.

ruin, till at length their fortune and their character
have sunk together, to rise no more. I do not say
that a man ought in every case to call his creditors
together the moment that he discovers he cannot pay
twenty shillings in the pound; but he certainly
ought to do it without delay, as soon as he ceases
to hope that he shall ultimately do so.

Every Christian tradesman *should be very watchful
against those artifices, violations of truth, and unfair
advantages, which many resort to in the disposal of
their articles.* It might indeed have become the general practice ; but tricks of trade, if contrary to truth
and honesty, are clear and flagrant violations of religious duty. No prevalence of custom can make
that right, which in itself is wrong. The standard
of a Christian's morality is the Bible ; and whatever
is opposed to that, he must avoid and abhor.

A tradesman who makes a profession of religion,
*should be most eminent for justice, truth, honour, and
generosity,* in all his dealings. His religion should
be seen in all his conduct. " I know nothing of
that man's creed," said a person of a religious
tradesman with whom he dealt, " because I never
asked him what he believed; but a more honoura
ble, punctual, generous tradesman, I never met
with in my life. I would as soon take *his word*
for a thousand pounds, as I would another man's
bond for a shilling. Whatever he promises he performs, and to the time also." This is adorning the
doctrine of God his Saviour in all things.

It is very dishonourable, when a Christian tradesman *is actuated by a spirit of envy and jealousy towards others,* and when he employs *ungenerous* means
to prevent their success. No one has an exclusive
monopoly, except in the case of patents. Others
have as much right to live where they like, as we

have.   It is *their world,* as well as ours ; and to employ our wealth in any case to ruin them, by *under-
selling,* is a spirit perfectly incompatible with the
genius of religion, and the nature of Christian fellowship.   Such an envious person deserves excommunication, not only from the church of God, but from
the society of rational creatures.

It is perfectly obvious, that the tradesman *ought to
regulate his expenditure by his income.*   The man that
lives beyond his resources is a robber and a thief.
His extravagance is supported by the property of
others ; and as it is taken without their consent,
it is a felony, for which he is answerable, if not
at the bar of man, yet certainly at the tribunal
of God.

CHAPTER IX.

MISCELLANEOUS SUBJECTS.

On the true Nature of Church Power.

In our conversation upon the subject of church
government, it is very common to talk of the power or authority of our churches.   But in what does
this power really consist, and how far does it extend ?
Every society has certainly an unquestionable right
to regulate all its own temporal and spiritual affairs,
to the entire exclusion of all *human* interference
and control whatever.   But we must be careful
not to carry the idea of independence so far as to
trench upon the dominion of Jesus Christ.   The
power of a church is simply a right to put their own
construction upon the laws of Christ, and to obey
his laws, in the way which they think will be most

agreeable to him. This is neither understood nor
remembered with as much distinctness as it should
be. Hence it is a very usual thing for churches
at their stated, or occasional meetings, to consider
themselves as met to *make* laws, and set in order
the affairs of the spiritual kingdom ; and a great
deal is said about "*our* church," and "the rules
that *we* have established in *our* church." Our
church!! How came it ours? The church is
Christ's. The rules *we* have established!! The
sole right of *making* laws, is with Him to whom the
church belongs. The church is a kingdom, of
which Christ is *sole* monarch, the New Testament
is his spiritual *code*, and all the power *we* have, is
to execute the laws which he has already established. In the whole business of church government,
we are to acknowledge the authority, and consider
ourselves as doing the will of Christ. Nothing is
left to *our* will, to *our* wisdom, to *our* caprice ; but
in all things we are to be guided by the law of Jesus, laid down in his word.

In the choice of officers, in the admission of members, in the exercise of discipline, we are not to
act upon views and principles of our *own*, but are
to be guided by those we find in the New Testament. We have no power to *legislate*, but merely
to *interpret* the law, and obey. When we meet,
Christ is in the midst of us, not only by his essential presence, but by his revealed will ; and every
authoritative voice is hushed, but that which speaks
to us from the sacred canon. When a member is
proposed, we are not to ask, "Is he such an one as
we think will add respectability to our communion?
is he of long standing in the ways of God ? is he
peculiar in his habits ?" but, "Is he such an one as
Christ has received ?" When a measure is submit-

ted for our adoption, we are not first to inquire into its policy, but whether it is in exact accordance with the general principles and spirit of the New Testament. Every act of church government must be an explicit acknowledgment of the authority of Jesus, as King in Zion, and an act of obedience to his laws.

It is impossible for this sentiment to be stated too frequently or too forcibly. It lays the axe to the root of all the errors on church government, which have crept into the world. The papacy, and the episcopacy, with other ecclesiastical corruptions, may be traced to a want of proper views of the nature' of church power. Let it once be admitted that a church of Christ has a right of *legislating* beyond what is written in the New Testament, and there is no such thing as limiting the exercise of this right, until the authority of Christ is superseded, and his church is converted into a mere secular institution.

On the Mode of Conducting Church Meetings.

Every well regulated church will have its solemn and stated meetings for conducting the business necessarily connected with its existence and progress. Many ministers have imbibed a prejudice against these meetings, and, like Charles the First, who, not finding the parliament as suppliant as he could wish. determined to govern without parliaments altogether, *they* have resolved to rule without calling the church together, except, at least, on extraordinary emergencies. I admit that church meetings have been abused ; but this has been more frequently the *fault of the pastor*, than the people. They have sometimes exhibited scenes of confusion, little recommendatory of the democratic form of church government. This, however, is not the error of the system, but the improper way in which it is administered. When ignorance or imprudence is elevated to the chair, order and decorum cannot be looked for in the assembly.

It would conduce to the order of church meetings, if it were much inculcated by the pastor, and generally understood by the people, that they were meetings for *devotion*, and not for *debate*. They should ever be attended with the usual services of a prayer meeting, i. e. with singing, supplication, and ministerial exhortation. If business is to be done, it should be thus introduced, and transacted in the spirit, and amidst the services of devotion. These times of assembling should be *periodical*; for when they are only occasional, they lose the character of devotional seasons, and assume the form of business meetings, to which the members come prepared for protracted and general discussion.

The admonition of the apostle is always in season, but never more so than in reference to the times of the assembling of the saints: " Let every man be slow to speak." And when any one does deliver his opinion, it should not be in a prating, dogmatical manner, but in few words, modestly spoken. Not only the pastor, but the people themselves, should discourage those forward, obtrusive spirits, to whom no music or melody is so pleasant as the sound of their own voice. *Talking* assemblies soon become *disorderly* ones. A wise and prudent minister will set his face against them; and a wise and prudent church will support him in this conduct.

It is, of course, no less the interest than the duty of the society, *to support, at all its meetings, the just and scriptural authority of the pastor.* He should never be addressed but in the most courteous and respectful manner, and every expression of rudeness should be marked with the disapprobation of the members present.

On the Admission of Members to the Church.

When an individual is known to be desirous of fellowship, information of this should be conveyed without delay to the pastor, who, upon conversing with the person, and making suitable inquiries about his character and conduct, may mention him as a candidate for fellowship. No member should bring forward a candidate in opposition to the opinion of the pastor. It is of course to be expected, that *he* will never reject an individual, but upon grounds which appear to him to be quite sufficient, and which he will, without hesitation or reserve, communicate to the person himself.

On the part of the church, there is sometimes a very unscriptural reluctance to receive persons into membership, till after they have had *a long trial of their Christian steadfastness and integrity.* It is very common for some members to exclaim in surprise, when the name of a candidate is mentioned to them in secret, "What, is *he* going to be proposed to the church? Why, he has not been converted three months." I wish these over-cautious Christians to tell me, what length of time *ought* to elapse after conversion, before the individual is introduced to communion? Has Jesus Christ stated any term of probation, which we must pass through before we are received into the church? Certainly not.

What right have *we* then to fix upon any? Is it
not establishing terms of communion, which *he* has
not established? Is not this a direct invasion of
his authority? If we consult the precedents furnished by the practice of the apostles, they most
decisively condemn the overstrained caution of
those, who would put a Christian upon the trial of
a year or two, before he is admitted to communion.
The very day in which a man professed himself a
Christian, he was added to the church. In fact,
his joining himself to the church, was his profession. I would have every step taken to inquire into the knowledge, faith, and conduct of an individual who proposes himself for fellowship; and if
they are satisfactory, I would admit him, although
he had been converted but a single month; and I
call upon the person who would refuse to join in
such admission, to show on what ground he acts.
Let him not talk about the necessity of caution,
and the possibility of being deceived; this is very
true, but it must not be allowed to interfere with
the rules which Christ has laid down for the government of his church. Our views of policy cannot improve his institutions, and ought not to oppose the practice of his apostles. The rule of our
proceeding is simply this, " We must receive those
whom we think the Lord hath received." Abandon this rule, and we have no directory for our
conduct. One person may think a year's trial
enough; but another may think two years' necessary. It is truly shocking to see how many excellent and exemplary Christians are kept by some
churches, month after month, at a distance from the
fellowship of the faithful, under the pretence of
trying their steadfastness. " We must not take the
13

children's bread," say these ultra cautious disciples, " and cast it to the dogs." Nor have you a right to *starve* the children, any more than you have to *pamper* the dogs. Our rule is this, " evidence of personal religion, whether that evidence be the result of a month or a year."

The Lord's supper is intended no less for babes than fathers in Christ; and who will contend that the right way to treat a new born infant, is to neglect him, and leave him to himself, to see whether he will live? To nurse and feed him are the ordained means to preserve his life. It is precisely the same in spirituals as in temporals. And if it be proper to say of a child that died in consequence of neglect, that he would have lived if proper care had been taken, it is not less correct to say of some persons that once appeared hopeful, but afterwards returned to the world, they would have proved honourable Christians, had they not been neglected by the church.

The same unscriptural caution is sometimes displayed towards those converts, who are *young in years.* It is surprising to see what a panic some members are thrown into, when a *young* person is proposed as a candidate for fellowship; and if they happen to discover that the youth is only fifteen or sixteen years of age, they seem to feel as if the church was either going to be profaned or destroyed. Is there, then, a *canonical age* of membership? Is the same rule established in the kingdom of Christ, which is observed in the kingdoms of the world, and every one considered as unfit for the privileges of citizenship, till he arrive at the age of one and twenty? If not, what right have *we* to speak or think about the *age* of a candidate? *Piety* is all we have to inquire into; and whether the individual be fourteen, or fourscore, we are to receive him, provided we have reason to suppose, "that Christ has received him."

The MODE OF ADMISSION is various in different churches. On this subject we have no other scriptural guide than mere general principles. The *church* is to receive the member, and any mode which they may adopt to ascertain the sincerity of his piety, is lawful, provided that it is not so rigid as to deter persons from applying for admission. In every case, the *church* ought to have the means of ascertaining the piety of the individuals; without this there can be no real communion. In some churches, the *pastor only* examines the candidate: but this is too great a power to delegate to any man, and too great a responsibility for any man willingly to incur. In other churches, the individuals are examined *before the body of the brethren.* Another plan is, for the *pastor and two of the brethren to converse with the candidate in private,* and then state their opinion to the assembled church. In addition to this, some churches require a *written statement* of the religious views and feelings of the candidate. To make this a *sine qua non* of admission, is unscriptural and absurd, since many cannot write at all, and others are so unaccustomed to commit their thoughts to writing, that their letters are so incoherent as to be scarcely fit to be read in public. It is admitted that there are some advantages connected with the plan.

It is deeply interesting to hear a simple, artless account of a sinner's conversion; and by his particularizing the very sermons which were the means of his conversion, he helps in no small degree to raise the pastor in the estimation of the church,

by these proofs of his usefulness and success, and
to endear him to their hearts.*

On Discipline.

By discipline, is meant, *the right treatment of offending members.* The church which neglects this
duty, resembles a state in which the administration
of justice is omitted, and crime is permitted to be
practised with impunity. That part of the design of
church union, which consists in mutual watchfulness,
is lost; backsliders are encouraged to go farther
astray, hypocrites are patronised in their self-delu-
sion, the ruin of men's souls abetted, the society is
corrupted, and the honour of religion is compromised.
It is this sin which the apostle describes in those
awful words, " If any man defile the temple of God,
him shall God destroy." The church is that temple, and to defile it, is to introduce improper members to its communion, or to tolerate them in the
practice of sin. The passage of Scripture which is
connected with the one I have just quoted, appears
to me to be very generally misunderstood, and in
its true meaning to be deserving of especial consideration, in reference to the subject of church discipline. " Now, if any man build upon this foundation, gold, silver, precious stones, wood, hay, stubble ; every man's work shall be made manifest.
For the day shall declare it, because it shall be revealed by fire ; and the fire shall try every man's

---

* In most of our American churches, candidates are required
to appear before the assembled church, and detail the methods
of grace by which God brought them to his knowledge and
service.   *Ed.*

work of what sort it is. If any man's work abide
which he hath built thereupon, he shall receive a
reward. If any man's work shall be burnt, he shall
suffer loss, but he himself shall be saved, yet so as
by fire." 1 Cor. iii. 12—15. It has been usual to
interpret this passage in reference to doctrines;
but the true view of it would refer it to persons.
The materials laid by different preachers are not
the sentiments which they preach, but the members
which they add to the church. The leaders of the
different sects in the Corinthian church, were under
the temptation of introducing improper persons to
the communion, with the view of increasing their
party. Now, says the apostle, this is building up
the temple of Christ with unsuitable materials,
and therefore defiling it with the admixture of
hay and stubble. The fire of persecution, however, would try every man's work; for the times
of suffering would be sure to drive off those false
professors, in whom the word had no root, and then
this bad workmanship would be utterly destroyed.
Let ministers and churches, therefore, beware of
that want of discipline, by which bad materials are
either added to, or kept in the walls of the spiritual
house, since his is the crime of defiling the temple
of God. To suffer offences to be committed from
time to time, without being noticed and removed,
must be as displeasing in the sight of God, as it
would have been, if the Jews had permitted any
filthy substances to remain in the temple of Solomon, or had swept the impurities of the sacrifices
into the holy of holies. A single unpunished trans-
gressor troubled the whole camp of Israel, and
brought calamity upon a nation; nor could the favour of God rest upon the people, till Achan was
discovered and destroyed. Nothing can be con-

ceived of, more likely to grieve the Holy Spirit, or to induce him to withdraw his gracious influence from a church, than a neglect of scriptural discipline. And it is worth while to examine, whether this is not one of the causes of the declining state of many Christian societies.

The advantages of discipline are obvious and numerous. It reclaims backsliders, it detects hypocrites, it circulates a secret and salutary awe through the church, supplies an additional incentive to watchfulness and prayer, by exhibiting at once the most affecting proofs of human frailty, and the painful consequences resulting from its exposure; while, in addition, it is a public testimony, borne by the church, against all unrighteousness.

Here several things deserve particular consideration.

I. What offences should become subject to discipline.

1. Of course, *all scandalous vices and immoralities.* "Not to keep company, if any man that is called a brother, be a fornicator, or covetous, or an idolater, or a railer, or a drunkard, or an extortioner, with such an one, no, not to eat,—put away from yourselves that wicked person," (mentioned verse 1,) 1 Cor. v. 11—13.

2. *The denial of essential articles of the Christian faith*, and persisting in the error.

"But though we, or an angel from heaven, preach any other gospel to you than that we have preached, let him be accursed." Gal. i. 8. "Of whom is Hymeneus and Philetus, who, concerning the truth, have erred, saying the resurrection is past already, and overthrow the faith of some—whom I deliver to Satan." 2 Tim. ii. 17—21. "If any man teach otherwise, and consent not to the words

of Christ and sound doctrine, according to godliness
—from such withdraw thyself." 1 Tim. vi. 3—5.
"If there come any unto you and bring not this
doctrine, receive him not into your house, neither bid
him God speed; for he that biddeth him God speed,
is a partaker of his deeds." 2 John 10, 11. Nothing
can be more plain than that these passages require
us to separate from our communion those who deny
what we consider to be the essential articles of our
faith. Every church has an indubitable right of determining for themselves, what they consider to be
fundamental truths; they should, however, be extremely cautious, not to set up other terms of communion than those which are established in the
Word of God. It is difficult to say, where forbearance should terminate, and discipline begin; but
there can be no doubt as to the path of duty, when
a member denies the divinity, atonement, and spiritual influence of our blessed Lord. With such a
person, it is impossible to have any spiritual communion, and we ought not to hold with him any
visible union. Reason as well as revelation for-
bids it.

3. *Disturbing the peace of the church in any way,*
is an offence that imperatively demands the exercise of discipline.

"A man that is a heretic,* after the first and
second admonition, reject." Titus iii. 10. " I
would they were cut off that trouble you." Gal. v.
12. "Mark them which cause divisions, and avoid
them." Rom. xvi. 17. "We command you, breth-

* The word here translated heretic signifies rather the author
and leader of a party, whatever his opinions may be, than one
who holds erroneous sentiments. It means a factious person,
who raises a sect in the society, whether the ground of their
association be a matter of feeling or opinion.

ren, in the name of our Lord Jesus Christ, that ye
withdraw yourselves from every brother that walks
disorderly." 2 Thess. iii. 6.

We are here taught, that if any man disturb the
peace, or break the unity of the church, no matter
in what way, whether by insinuating that the pastor does not preach the gospel, or by forming a
party against him, or by raising up a division to oppose the proceedings of the society in a factious and
contentious manner, he must without delay be dealt
with as an offender. He may be a moral, and in
appearance a holy man, but this is not to screen
him from discipline: on the contrary, these very
qualities enable him, if suffered to continue, to do
the greater mischief. A *factious temper*, when
united with reputed sanctity, is the most dangerous
character that can exist in a Christian society. An
immoral man can do little harm: his vices have a
repellent power to drive away from him all who
have a regard for their own reputation; but a man
who, under the guise of piety, becomes a troubler
of Israel, will be a troubler *indeed*. He should be
instantly called to account for his conduct, and if
not reclaimed by mild and affectionate admonition,
separated from communion. As long as the church
contains such an individual, it is cherishing a viper
in its bosom.

4. *Suffering near relatives to want the necessaries
of life, when able to relieve them.*

"If any man provide not for his own house, he
hath denied the faith, and is worse than an infidel."
1 Tim. v. 8.

5. *Living in a state of irreconcilable enmity with
any of the brethren, and refusing to make suitable
concessions for an injury inflicted.* "If he will not

hear the church, let him be unto thee as an heathen man and a publican." Matt. xviii. 17.

II. The manner of proceeding in cases of discipline.

There are many things, of which no other notice should be taken than the private admonition of one member to another. When the offence is comparatively trivial, and known only to an individual or two, nothing more is necessary than for these individuals, without saying a syllable about the matter to any one else, to go, in a spirit of great meekness and affection, to the offender, and to admonish him. It is very undesirable to bring any thing more into our church meetings than is absolutely necessary. If the sin be attended with much aggravation, and be generally known, it is a duty to mention it to the church.* Should the offender confess the fact, and manifest satisfactory proofs of contrition, a simple and affectionate admonition to him to go and sin no more, is sufficient. The church should be satisfied, and restore him forthwith to their confidence. But if he be obstinate—if he either deny the charge, or palliate his sin—it would be proper to appoint two or three discreet individuals to inquire into the fact, and to endeavour to bring him to repentance. At the time the deputation is appointed, a resolution ought to be passed, suspending the individual from the privileges of communion.† Time after time he should be visited

---

* See p. 84, where the author treats of *private offences.* *Ed.*

† The suspension from the table, which is denominated the lesser excommunication, is opposed by some as a measure that has no Scripture warrant. But may it not, like many other of our practices, be fairly deduced from general principles, and be as proper as though it were expressly enjoined? Does not reason and the very nature of things require it? Is there no

by the pastor, and admonished; and if after one, or two, or three months, he should confess his offence, and discover satisfactory contrition, he should without delay be restored to the confidence and communion of the church. But after waiting a reasonable time, and waiting in vain, for any marks of repentance, the church should proceed to separate him

---

medium between a mere admonition and the awful extremity of expulsion? What is to be done in those cases, where neither the guilt nor the innocence of an individual is at once apparent to the church; but still a strong, very strong case, so far as *prima farie* evidence goes, is made out against him; or where there is some appearance of penitence, but yet that penitence is equivocal? Are we to admit that individual to the full privileges of communion? what, while his conduct is under examination, and his character, to say the best, suspicious? It is useless to affirm that he is innocent till proved guilty; this may do in worldly matters, where no communion of heart is necessary; but not in the church of God, where the very act of sitting down at the sacred table is an expression of mutual confidence, esteem, and love. Besides, even in civil affairs, a man is denied the rights of innocence before he is proved guilty; I mean during the interval between his arrest and trial. He is then in a state of suspension. Analogous to his is the case of a suspected member, and who must therefore be suspended till proved innocent or penitent. Still more culpable would it be to proceed to excommunication, while there are signs of penitence, even though those signs were not quite satisfactory. Exclude the act of suspension from discipline, and the churches will often be involved in the dilemma of either having their confidence impaired by retaining suspicious members, or being obliged to expel those who are not so hopeless as to be consigned to this awful condition. To say that they may be admitted again as soon as they are proved to be penitent, is to destroy the salutary terrors of a sentence, which ought not to be pronounced, but in the last extremity, and the solemnity of which nothing should be allowed to impair.

[*Note.*—As differences of opinion exist relative to the propriety of suspension, churches, in this respect, are not uniform in their practice. **Ed.**]

from their communion. His contumacy has immeasurably aggravated his original offence. He has now resisted, pertinaciously, the command and will of Christ, declared through the church, and must be treated as a heathen man and a publican. If he neglect to hear the church, he must, whatever might have been his original transgression, be expelled from its fellowship.

In some cases, where the crime is highly scandalous, and very notorious, it is necessary for the honour of religion, the credit of the society, and the good of the offender, to proceed immediately to excommunication, as soon as the fact is clearly proved.

By excommunication, we mean nothing more than an entire separation of the offender from all relation to the church whatever, and an utter exclusion from its privileges. The solemn sentence is purely spiritual, designed to maintain the purity of the church, and to manifest the glory of Christ's holiness in the government of his kingdom, and cannot extend to the person, estate, liberty, or any civil rights whatever, of the excluded members.*

---

* There is some difficulty, and consequently has been much dispute, about the precise import of the apostle's expression, 1 Cor. v. 5. "To deliver such an one unto Satan for the destruction of the flesh." The same expression is used in reference to Hymeneus and Philetus, 1 Tim. i. 20. "Whom I have delivered unto Satan, that they may learn not to blaspheme." Some have supposed, that nothing more is intended than their being delivered over again to the kingdom of Satan, from which they were translated into the kingdom or church of Christ. In other words, that they were sent back again to the state of unconverted men, to be subject to the usurped dominion of the god of this world, and led captive by him at his will. But I do not see how by this means they were to learn "not to blaspheme," or to have " the flesh destroyed," which are stat-

The sentence of excommunication should never be proceeded to by the church, but with the greatest caution and seriousness; it should be accompanied with sorrowful and humble confession of the delinquent's sin, and earnest prayer that it may have a suitable effect upon *his* mind, and the mind of others; it should be done in the name of the Lord Jesus, and not as an act of the church's own authority; it should have an immediate reference to the ends of church fellowship, and the benefit of the offender; it should be unattended by any emotions of wrath, malice, party spirit, or personal resentment; in short, from the beginning to the end of the fearful proceeding, there should be a manifestation of all that deliberation, discretion, seriousness, grief, and awe, which this solemn act of excision seems naturally to demand.   There appears in

---

ed by the Apostle, as the end and design of his thus dealing with them. To get over this, some have supposed that the offender's pride, lust, and other fleshly passions, would be mortified when he found himself despised and shunned by all. This view of the case is rather far-fetched, and does not agree so well with the more natural interpretation of the words given by others, nor with the threatenings denounced by the Apostle in other places. 1 Cor. iv. 21. 2 Cor. xiii. 1. It is certain the Apostles had power to punish notorious offenders with disease and death. If so, may we not believe that the command which the Apostle gave on this occasion to the Corinthians, "to deliver the incestuous person to Satan for the destruction of his flesh," was an exertion of that power? The only difficulty which occurs in regard to this interpretation is, that it ascribes to Satan an instrumentality in the infliction of disease, which is no where acknowledged in the word of God. More than hints, however, are to be found both in the Old Testament and New, that such an influence is possessed by him. The case of Job, and the woman whose case is mentioned, Luke xiii. 16, "whom Satan hath bound, lo, these eighteen years," are quite in point.

this act, a reference to the future judgment of Christ. In one sense, the church now judges for Christ in matters of his kingdom; and wo to them who dare to pronounce this sentence, without being persuaded on good grounds, that it is the sentence of Christ himself. It is the echo of his awful voice, saying even now to the offender, " Depart from my house ;" and unless the offender repent, an antici- pation of his sentence, saying at the last day, " De- part from my heaven."

Mr. Hall's description of the nature and useful- ness of excommunication is very striking. " I am far from thinking lightly of the spiritual power with which Christ has armed his church. It is a high and mysterious one, which has no parallel on earth. Nothing in the order of means, is equally adapted to awaken compunction in the guilty, with spiritual censures impartially administered ; the sentence of excommunication in particular, harmonizing with the dictates of conscience, and re-echoed by her voice, is truly terrible. It is the voice of God, speaking through its legitimate organ, which he who despises, or neglects, ranks with ' heathen men and publicans,' joins the synagogue of Satan, and takes his lot with an unbelieving world, doomed to perdition. Excommunication is a sword, which, strong in its apparent weakness, and the sharper, and the more keenly edged, for being divested of all sensible and exterior envelopements, lights im- mediately on the spirit, and inflicts a wound which no balm can cure, no ointment can mollify, but which must continue to ulcerate and burn, till heal- ed by the blood of atonement, applied by penitence and prayer. In no instance is that axiom more ful- ly verified, ' The weakness of God is stronger than men, and the foolishness of God is wiser than men,'

than in the discipline of his church.   By encumber-
ing it with foreign aid, they have robbed it of its
real strength ; by calling in the aid of temporal
pains and penalties, they have removed it from the
spirit to the flesh, from its contact with eternity, to
unite it to secular interests ; and, as the corruption
of the best things is the worst, have rendered it the
scandal and reproach of our holy religion.

" While it retains its character as a spiritual ordinance, it is the chief bulwark against the disorders which threaten to overrun religion, the very
nerve of virtue, and, next to the preaching of the
cross, the principal antidote to the ' corruptions that
are in the world through lust.'   Discipline in a
church occupies the place of laws in a state : and
as a kingdom, however excellent its constitution,
will inevitably sink into a state of extreme wretch-
edness, in which laws are either not enacted, or not
duly administered ; so a church which pays no attention to discipline, will either fall into confusion,
or into a state so much worse, that little or nothing
remains worth regulating.   The right of inflicting
censures, and of proceeding in extreme cases to
excommunication, is an essential branch of that
power with which the church is endowed, and bears
the same relation to discipline that the administration of criminal justice bears to the general principles of government.   When this right is exerted in
upholding the ' faith once delivered to the saints,'
or enforcing a conscientious regard to the laws of
Christ, it maintains its proper place, and is highly
beneficial.   Its cognizance of doctrine is justified
by apostolic authority; ' a heretic, after two or
three admonitions, reject :' nor is it to any purpose
to urge the difference betwixt ancient heretics and

modern, or that to pretend to distinguish truth from error, is a practical assumption of infallibility."

It is a question worthy of consideration, "How church members should *conduct themselves toward those who are thus separated from their communion.*" We are not left without instructions on this head. "If any man obey not our word by this epistle, note that man, and have no company with him, that he may be ashamed. Yet count him not as an enemy, but admonish him as a brother." 2 Thes. iii. 14, 15. "I have written unto you, not to keep company, if any man that is called a brother, be a fornicator, or covetous, or an idolater, or a railer, or a drunkard, or an extortioner, with such an one, no, not to eat." 1 Cor. v. 11. Two things are here evident: first—We are expressly commanded *to withdraw from all voluntary association* with such individuals. We are to shun their company. We are not even to sit down with them at an ordinary meal, nor freely to converse with them on secular affairs, except they are our relations, or we are necessarily thrown by the contingencies of business into their society. Of course, none of the relative ties are to be dissolved, nor any of the social duties to be neglected; but all *voluntary* intercourse with excommunicated persons, who are not related to us by the ties of nature, is to be cautiously avoided: and this is to be done, to testify our abhorrence of the sin, and that the offender himself may be ashamed, and feel the awful situation in which his transgression has placed him.

But it is equally evident from the apostolic injunction, that excommunicated persons are not to be *utterly forsaken and abandoned.* "Count him not as an enemy, but admonish him as a brother." Pains should be taken to bring them to repentance.

They should not be given up to their sins, and given over, as it were, to become more and more vile. The pastor and members should seek opportunities to admonish and warn them: "Peradventure God may give them repentance to the acknowledging of the truth." Upon their penitence and reformation, they should again be received into communion with compassion and love, joy and gratitude. "Better," says Dr. Owen, "never excommunicate a person at all, than forsake and abandon him when he is expelled, or refuse to receive him back again upon his repentance; but there is a class of persons unto whom, if a man be an offender, he shall be so for ever."

Great care should be taken by a church, to *display the most inflexible* IMPARTIALITY in the exercise of discipline. To allow the riches, talents, or influence of any offender, to blind the eyes of the society, and to screen him from punishment, is a most flagrant crime against the authority of Christ, and the laws of his kingdom. We can scarcely conceive of any thing more displeasing in his sight, any thing more likely to bring down his fearful indignation upon a church, than to allow his temple to be defiled, *out of compliment to secular distinctions.*

No member should be allowed to *resign, in order to avoid expulsion.* If he has done any thing worthy of censure or separation, he should not be allowed to retire with his conduct unnoticed. "It becomes not the wisdom and order of any society, intrusted with authority for its own preservation, as the church is by Christ himself, to suffer persons obnoxious to censure by the fundamental rules of that society, to cast off all respect unto it, to break their order and relation, without animadverting thereupon, according to the authority wherewith they are intrusted. To do otherwise is to expose their order unto contempt, and proclaim a diffidence in their own authority for the spiritual punishment of offenders."*

On the Removal of Members from one Church to another in the same Town.

This of course can happen only in those places where there are more than one church of the same denomination, and in such places it is a very common occurrence. Church fellowship is a very sacred bond, which ought not to be formed without serious deliberation, nor broken without just cause. No member should dissolve his connexion with a Christian society, but upon such grounds as will stand the test of reason and revelation. The slight pretexts on which some persons transfer themselves from one church to another, betrays a frivolity and volatility of mind, which looks like trifling with sacred things. On the least offence, either imaginary or real, produced either by minister or people, they send for their dismission to another communion, and are off.

Sometimes *a disagreement with one of the members* is the cause of secession. This is manifestly wrong. The scripture is very explicit on the subject of offences. Instead of leaving a church on this ground, we ought to take immediate steps towards reconciliation. It is no justification to say, " If I cannot sit down at the Lord's Supper in love with a person, I had better not sit down at all;" because we ought without delay to have the offence

---

* Dr. Owen on Church Government, p. 222.
14

removed, and come to an agreement with the offender.

Some persons break their connexion with a church, because they think that *there are sinful members retained in its communion.* Instead of removing, their duty is, either by private admonition, to reclaim such supposed delinquents, or, by informing the pastor, to take the proper measures for their expulsion. If the matter should be brought before the church, and the brethren should not be convinced that there is sufficient ground to proceed to discipline, we ought immediately to acquiesce, and to suppose that through want of information, or some secret prejudice, we had formed an incorrect opinion; and from that time should feel charitably toward the individuals in question. And even if we were persuaded that the church had erred in its judgment, yet, as they examined the evidence, and acted upon conviction, it is not our duty to retire. They endeavoured to decide impartially, and as they did not *connive* at wickedness, their communion is not defiled. Societies must be governed by fixed general laws, which may sometimes fail to reach particular cases. We must always act upon evidence; and if this fail to prove a member guilty, we must still consider ourselves bound to continue him in the privileges of communion.

If a church *refuses to take cognizance of flagrant immorality,* or, in order to screen some rich and powerful member, *declines to receive testimony,* or acts *in direct opposition to the clearest evidence,*—a case which rarely happens,—then the communion is defiled, and a member may conscientiously withdraw.

It happens not unfrequently that members secede, *because a pastor is chosen, whose election they cannot approve.* This forms a difficult case of casuistry. It ought, however, to be a last resort. We should never form a separation on this ground in haste. We should give a patient and impartial hearing to the minister, and strive, by every possible effort, to have our prejudices removed. We should not suffer ourselves to be disaffected towards him, by circumstances trivial and indifferent. We should not lend our ear to those who have similar views, nor suffer a party feeling to be excited; but, acting singly and for ourselves, strive to edify so far by his ministry, as to render a secession unnecessary. If, however, after earnest prayer for direction, coupled with great efforts to subdue every thing of prejudice, we still find our religious edification not promoted by his preaching, then we may quietly and peaceably retire, provided there are numbers and property sufficient to found another congregation, and erect another place of worship. We should never attempt to prejudice the minds of others; a step which is not unfrequently taken by some to justify their own conduct; but which is attended with more guilt than words can describe.

It is quite unlawful to separate merely on the ground of *dissatisfaction with the decision of the church, in its ordinary affairs.*

It is equally sinful to retire because of *some imaginary or real offence given us by the pastor.* The same steps of explanation and reconciliation are to be taken in this case, as in that of a private member. We should go to him alone, but in the spirit of the greatest meekness and respect, on account of his office. Nothing should be said in the way of accusation, crimination, or demand; but a kind, respectful, modest statement of the supposed offence should be given, which, with any reasonable man, will be always sufficient to lead to a satisfactory explanation.

A member ought not to retire, even on the ground of *supposed misconduct* on the part of the pastor. If his inconsistencies affect his Christian character, they should become matter of church investigation : if they are but imprudences, or the lighter imperfections to which even the best of men are subject, we should be rather disposed to treat them with all reasonable candour, and cover them with the veil of love ; at the same time it would be proper, that a respectful and kind expostulation should be delivered to him by the deacons, or senior members of his flock.

In cases where a newly married couple are members of two churches, *it is quite lawful* for the wife to withdraw from her own church to that of her husband, provided she can edify by his minister ; if not, the husband ought not to desire her to accompany him. If by a removal of our dwelling place, we are situated at an inconvenient distance from the house of God, it is quite justifiable, in this case, to connect ourselves with a religious society nearer to our abode ; but then we ought to withdraw altogether, and not hear the word preached in one place, and receive the Lord's supper in another. This practice is very common in the metropolis, than which, I think, nothing can be more opposed to the very spirit of church fellowship. This is resolving the whole Christian communion into the mere act of celebrating the Lord's supper ; whereas this is but one part of it. It is destructive of many ends of fellowship. It interferes with pastoral inspection ; for how can a minister judge of a member's regular attendance upon the ordinances of religion, when he sees him only once a month at the table of the

Lord ? It also interrupts the growth of brotherly love, which is promoted by frequent association in the public ordinances of religion.

Let us then consider that our connexion with a Christian church is a bond of a very sacred nature, and which, though not indissoluble, should not be broken but upon some great and rare occurrence.

On the Conduct to be observed by a Church in the Election of a Pastor.

When a Christian minister is removed either to his eternal rest, or to some other sphere of labour in the present world, the choice of a successor always brings on a crisis in the history of the church of which he was the pastor. No event that could happen, can place the interests of the society in greater peril. Distraction and division have so frequently resulted from this circumstance, so many churches have been rent by it, that an argument has been founded upon it, if not against the *right* of popular election to the pastoral office, yet against the expediency of using it. It must be admitted that, on these occasions, our principles as independents, and our practices as Christians, have not been unfrequently brought into disrepute. We have been accused of wrangling about a *teacher* of religion, till we have lost our religion itself in the affray ; and the state of many congregations proves, that the charge is not altogether without foundation. God sometimes overrules these divisions for the furtherance of the gospel, even as he has made the introduction of evil into the moral world, an occasion of displaying his glory ; but this alters not the character of the event. Schisms are altogether evil in themselves, and are always to be deprecated, and, if possible, avoided. This occurrence forms no solid objection, however, against the great principle —the right of every Christian to choose his own spiritual instructer. We must carefully separate, in a system, between what is accidental, and what is essential; and if, through the infirmity of our nature, some evils of an adventitious kind arise in the administration of a system clearly founded on reason and revelation, we are no more authorized to subvert the latter on account of the former, than we should be to demolish a hospital, in order to suppress the litigations which arise in its committee, about the direction of its concerns. What we have to do in one case and the other, is to leave the institution untouched, and endeavour to avoid these evils, which arise from our imperfections, to obscure its excellence, and limit its benefits.

Under these views, I shall proceed to point out in what way a church should conduct itself, when called upon to exercise its right in the choice of a minister.

Let all the members, as soon as their pastor is removed or dead, *seriously reflect on the crisis into which the church is brought*, the great importance of preserving its peace, and the influence that their individual conduct may have upon the future prosperity of the society. Let them deliberately reflect thus, " The church is now coming into circumstances of peril, and I, as an individual, may be accessory, according as my conduct shall be to its injury or prosperity. God forbid our harmony should be disturbed, or our Zion become otherwise than a quiet habitation. So far as depends upon myself, I will sacrifice any thing but principle, rather than have those scenes of distraction and division amongst us, which are so common in the religious world."

Let the members instantly *make it an object of fervent and constant prayer, that the church may be kept in harmony and peace,* guided in the choice of a minister, and that they may be enabled, each in his private capacity, to conduct himself in a spirit of quietness and brotherly love. Each one alone should pray for the Christian temper; and *periodical seasons* should be appointed, when these objects should be recognised, and their desires expressed by *social* prayer. Prayer is the best bulwark against strifes. The spirit of healing and union descends in the cloud of incense formed by the church's prayers.

Let the members recollect, that the choice of a pastor is one of those occasions, *which render pre-eminently necessary, the exercise of that* LOVE which St. Paul has so beautifully described in the first Epistle to the Corinthians. This chapter should be devoutly read at every church meeting, together with the 122d and the 133d Psalms. These should form the standing lessons for the occasion. The business now under consideration will require on all hands the utmost caution, candour, patience, and mutual forbearance. Many opinions are now to be consulted, many tempers to be tried, and each one should subject the passions of his own mind to the government of the word of God. If LOVE were elevated to the throne of the church, all would go right. No division would then take place. Difference of opinion might be expressed, but it would produce no alienation of heart. Directly therefore as it becomes necessary to elect a new pastor, the relationship of the church *as brethren,* and the *new commandment* of Christ, as the law of his kingdom, should, by a solemn act of the church, be recognised afresh.

The members should *study St. Paul's Epistles to Timothy and Titus*, to learn what are the qualifica-tions of a Christian minister.   They should well consider and settle with themselves, what objects should direct their choice.   It appears to me, they should unite in their view, *personal edification*, and *general benefit*.   They should seek for a man whom *they* can hear with pleasure, and who is likely *to prove attractive to others.*   The benefit of the society at large, is the ultimate standard, to which private and personal taste must ever give way.

A committee, composed of the deacons, or of the deacons and a few of the most judicious members, should be appointed to procure supplies, and look out for candidates.   This committee should write to the most discreet and esteemed ministers in their neighbourhood, or at a distance, who may be best acquainted with the circumstances of the destitute church, to name any person or persons who, in their judgment, may be eligible as its future pastor.   To ask advice is not to solicit imposition.   And in such an affair as this, *not* to ask advice, is to betray a want of prudent caution, most censurable in itself, and often most injurious in its consequences.   At the same time, there are so many motives which in-fluence people in giving advice, that no church should be guided implicitly in their choice of a pas-tor by the opinions of others.   Whoever may be recommended, the church should exercise its own judgment as to the fitness of the person recom-mended; for want of this, I have known mistakes committed of the most lamentable nature.*

---

* Let ministers to whom applications are made by a destitute church, to recommend them a candidate, beware of suffering

Great care should be taken by those to whom the church has delegated the power of procuring candidates, *not to invite, upon probation, any individual of whose suitableness they have not received previous and satisfactory testimony.* Let it by no means be thought necessary *to wait long after the decease of a pastor,* before a successor is elected. Respect for *his* memory does not require that the pulpit should be continued vacant, or that the weeds of widowhood should be worn by the church for any given period. When an officer falls in battle, the welfare of the army requires that a successor should be *immediately* appointed.

Neither is it necessary, that a church *should hear a great variety of candidates,* before an election is made. To set out with the intention of hearing many, in order to choose one, is of all plans the most injudicious and mischievous. The very idea

themselves to mention the name of any individual, whom, in their conscientious opinion, they do not think to be suitable. To recommend any person out of mere pity, because he is destitute of a situation, or out of natural affection or friendship, because he happens to be a relative or acquaintance, without regard to his character, general qualifications, or such ableness for the situation in question, is a most criminal act, and deserves the severest reprobation. It is an act of the most guilty treachery towards, not an individual, but a community; not in reference to temporal interests, but to spiritual and eternal ones. In some cases, unsuitable recommendations are given from a love of patronage; in others, from an excess of good nature; but from whatever cause they proceed, the mischief they do is incalculable. Oftentimes the evil cures itself, as it respects the particular individuals, for their imprimatur to a cure, or their testimonial to a person, is so easily and so generally procured, is so indiscriminately and so lavishly given, that with all persons of discernment it really stands for nothing. Every man is responsible to God for all the evil consequences which result from a recommendation carelessly given.

15

that others are to follow, will suspend the impartial. exercise of the judgment concerning every one, will in all probability lead to a variety of opinions, and ensure a repetition of the state of things at Corinth, where one said, "I am for Paul; another, I am for Apollos; and a third, I am for Cephas." As soon as an individual is found who possesses the scriptural qualifications of a Christian pastor, and in whom the great body of the church is united, he should be immediately chosen, even if he be the first that has presented himself.

Great caution, however, ought to be exercised *in forming a judgment upon the suitableness of an individual.* That a proper opportunity might be afforded to the church for coming to this opinion, the probationary term of a candidate's labours should not be *too short.* Preaching is not the only thing to be judged of; piety, prudence, diligence, general deportment, are all to be taken into the account: and for a trial on all these points, a period of *three months* cannot be thought too long.

Especial deference should be paid by the younger and inexperienced members of the church, to the opinion of their senior and more experienced brethren. The sentiments of the deacons, and those individuals who have grown grey in the service of the Lord and the church, should be received with great attention, and have great weight. A youth of seventeen is a very incompetent judge of ministerial qualifications, compared with a venerable father of seventy. That haughty spirit which leads a young person, or a novice, to say, "I have a vote as well as the oldest and richest, and have as much right to be heard and consulted as they," is not the spirit of the gospel, but of turbulence and faction. How much more amiable and lovely is such a declaration as the following: "I, young and in-experienced, am a very inadequate judge of the suitableness of a minister for this situation, and therefore shall be pretty much guided, in my decis-ion, by the opinion of others, older and wiser than myself." This *is independency exercised in the spirit of the gospel.*

All *secret canvassing*, and attempts to influence the minds of others, should be studiously avoided. To see the mean, petty arts of a contested election carried into the church of God, is dreadful.

It would be well for every church to have a standing rule, *that no pastor should be chosen, but by the suffrages of two thirds, or three fourths, of the members present.* This would preclude much of that cabal and intrigue, which are sometimes em-ployed in cases where the matter is decided by a mere majority. Besides which, the choice of a pas-tor is a business of too much importance to be car-ried simply by a majority.

It would be well, if in every case the church could be *unanimous;* but this is more than can be looked for. It should certainly be sought for in the use of all proper means. The majority should ex-ercise peculiar FORBEARANCE and AFFECTION to-wards those who are opposed to them, carefully avoiding to impute their objections to any improper motives; listening to their statements with pa-tience; treating them with candour; reasoning with them in the spirit of love; and giving them time to have their difficulties removed. The hap-piest results have been often the issue of such kind and Christian conduct. If, however, instead of this, the dissentients are treated with harshness and in-tolerance; if their opposition be attributed to a fac-tious and cavilling temper; if they are regarded with contempt, as a despicable minority, of which no notice should be taken; and are left immediately to themselves, without any conciliatory measures being taken, while the majority proceeds immediately to decide, a schism is sure to be the consequence, as mischievous to the church as it is disgraceful to religion.

The party who wish a minister to be elected, should seriously reflect thus: "If we choose this man, we may give pain to the minds of a large body of our brethren, which we most anxiously deprecate, and cannot allow ourselves to do, but under the conviction that we are promoting the permanent welfare of the church at large." While the party opposing should say, "The general body appear to consider this minister as possessing the requisite qualification for their pastor, and this has been so satisfactorily ascertained, that it ought not to be with us a light matter to obstruct the general edification. Nothing but the good of the church shall lead us to set up our opinion in opposition to that of a large majority of its members." Such a lovely temper would generally lead to beneficial results.

It would be very advisable, in some cases, for even so large a majority as two thirds, or even three fourths, *to give up the point*, rather than carry it in opposition to a minority, which includes in it the deacons, and many of the most experienced and respectable members of the society. The majority, in such instances, have the *right* to decide; but it is a question whether they ought not, for the sake of peace, to waive the exercise of it.

Persons of property and influence should be very careful how they conduct themselves on these occasions.
There are in many churches individuals whose

circumstances must necessarily give peculiar weight
to their opinions.   Let them, however, not assume
the office of dictators.   Let them not robe themselves in the dress of Diotrephes, nor display
amongst the brethren the love of preeminence.   The
system of independency admits of influence, but
not of patronage; men may lead, but not drive.
Democracies are as liable to the control of a few
leading individuals, probably more so, than any other
system; but then these individuals should act, *by
causing the people to act for them.*   If such an application of the words of scripture were admissible, I
would say, "they should render *the people willing* in
the day of their power."   An attempt to exert their
influence, in *opposition* to the wishes of the people,
is a most irrational, unscriptural assumption of power.   To sacrifice the interests of the church for the
gratification of their taste; to attempt to force upon a society a man not approved by it, or to reject
one who is chosen by it, is the most disgusting exercise of the most disgusting tyranny.

   It unfortunately happens, that when one party
has given up a minister in compliment to the other,
they almost insensibly *oppose an individual, who, in
future, may be the favourite of their opponents.*   It is
most sinful to allow the corrupt passions of our nature thus far to prevail in our hearts, as to turn
aside our judgment in affairs so sacred and so important.

   When a minister is at length brought in by a
large majority, it then becomes a question, *what
ought to be the conduct of the minority.*   Should they
separate, and form another religious society?   Certainly not, except as a dernier resort.   Let them
consider the evils connected with such a state of
things.   What ill will is often produced between

the two societies; how much anti-christian feeling
is excited; how it injures the spirit of both parties;
what envies, and jealousies, and evil speakings, com-
mence and continue, to the injury of religion, and
the triumph of its enemies! Let them, before they
separate, endeavour *to lay aside their prejudice*, and
hear for a season, with as much impartiality as possible, the man to whom they object. On *his* part,
much *consummate prudence* is necessary, and the
most conciliatory conduct. All he does and says
should have a healing tendency. Much depends
upon himself. Great credit is due to that minister,
WHO HAS CONCILIATED HIS OPPONENTS WITHOUT
ALIENATING HIS FRIENDS, and who has become THE
RECONCILING MEDIUM OF TWO PARTIES, ONCE AT
VARIANCE ABOUT HIMSELF.

In some cases, *a division is necessary*. Where
this is unavoidable, great efforts should be made to
effect it in *love*. If the two parties cannot *unite* in
peace, at least let them *separate* in peace. Let the
separation take place without alienation. Alas!
that this should so rarely be the case!

What we want, to preserve the peace of our
churches unbroken, is a more distinct recognition and
a more powerful influence of *the principles of the gospel;* more humility, more spirituality, more zeal for
the divine glory. We carry into the sanctuary, and
into the church, our pride, our self-will, our personal
taste. That spirit of mutual submission, brotherly love,
and surrender of our own gratification to the good
of others which the word of God enjoins, and our profession avows, would keep the church always happy
and harmonious, and enable it to pass in safety
through the most critical circumstances in which it
can be placed. Instead of seeking the good of the
whole, the feeling of too many of our members may

be thus summarily expressed—" I will have my way."
Such a spirit is a source of all the evils to which
our churches are ever exposed, and of which it
must be confessed they are but too frequently the
miserable victims.

*On the Propriety of occasionally administering the
Lord's Supper in private Houses, for the Sake of
sick Persons who are incapable of attending the
Solemnities of Public Worship.*

I do not now allude to the practice, so common
in the church of England, of administering the sacrament to *dying* persons, as a preparative for eternity ; this custom, so unscriptural in its nature, and
so delusory in its tendency, is unknown, I believe,
amongst our churches. But instances have occurred, in which our ministers, for the sake of some
of their members, who have been long confined to
their own habitations by chronic diseases, without
the prospect of ever going to the house of God
again, have assembled a few others in the chamber
of the afflicted person, and administered to them the
Lord's supper. The infirm individual is supposed
to be a real Christian, in church fellowship; the
others, joining in the act, are also members of the
same church, or Christians of undoubted piety ; and
the design of the act is not to countenance any
pharisaic notions of human merit, which the sick
person might have connected with the reception of
the sacrament, but simply to give him an opportunity of expressing his obedience, and gratifying his
love to Christ, by an observance of our Lord's
own institution. Is it right under these circumstances to gratify his request, and observe with

him the sacred supper? I think not; and on the following grounds:

1. The Lord's supper is strictly a *church ordinance*, and not an exercise of *mere social religion*, such as joint prayer, and therefore ought not to be observed but when the church is professedly assembled. It is not an act of social religion, which may be performed in any place, where two or three Christians are convened together, by accident or design, but in the place of their public convention, and at the time when they are so convened. All the directions of the apostle, concerning this institution, are given to the church in its collective capacity; and besides this, there are many incidental expressions, which plainly show that this was the view which he took of it, under the guidance of the Holy Ghost. In the eleventh chapter of the first epistle to the Corinthians, he interferes to regulate the abuses which, upon this subject, had crept into the Corinthian church. He begins the subject thus: "When ye come together in one place, this is not to eat the Lord's supper." Now his meaning in this language must evidently be, that merely coming into one place together for a feast, was not enough, but in that one place conforming to all the other regulations delivered by our Lord concerning it. The act of coming together in one place was right so far as it went, but it was not enough. In 1 Cor. v. 8, the apostle says, "Let us keep the feast," i. e. the Lord's supper, "not with old leaven:" in the 7th verse they were commanded to purge out the old leaven, i. e. to put away the offending member; and this was to be done when they were gathered together; the feast was to be observed then, when the church were gathered together.

It is plain therefore that the Lord's supper is a

church ordinance, and can with propriety be only
observed by the church in its assembled form.
But it will probably be said, "Do not two or three
persons convened together at any time, or in any
place, constitute a church?" The answer to this
question depends on circumstances. If these two
or three meet together for the purposes, and in the
character, of a distinct and separate society of
Christians, and in the usual time and place of assembly, they *are* a church, notwithstanding the
smallness of their number; but if they meet together as the acknowledged members of another society, which in its general capacity neither do, nor
can, assemble with them in that place, they are not
a church, but merely a part of one; and, as such,
have no right to perform acts which belong to the
whole number. This does not imply that it is necessary for every member to be present, in order to a
meeting of the church; for, provided all be invited to
assemble in one place, those who meet constitute
the church, however few may attend. This may
be illustrated by a reference to the British parliament. Two or three members, meeting together in
one place, do not constitute the senate, nor are
their acts legislatorial. The parliament are the
members assembled by appointment, whether few or
many, in the specified place of meeting. Such is
the church, not a casual, ambulatory, or private
meeting of a few of its members, but the body of
Christians convened by general notice. The
words of Christ, "Wherever two or three are gathered together in my name, there am I in the midst
of them," more immediately refer to the exercise
of social prayer; but, viewed in their most extensive sense, will by no means countenance the idea,
that two or three members of a church constitute

of themselves a church, until they have separated from their late connexion, and formed themselves into another distinct society.

2. The practice in question is contrary to one of the ends of the Lord's supper, which is to be a visible sign of the oneness of the church, of the union of *all* its members in *one* body. Hence said the apostle, " We being many are one bread (*loaf*) and one body ; for we are all partakers of that one bread (*loaf*.)" 1 Cor. x. 17. The loaf by its unity shows the oneness of the church; by its division into many parts, its many members. But is not this design of the Lord's supper defeated by its private celebration amongst a *few* members of the church? Are the two or three assembled in private, detached from the public body, a representation of its unity?

3. There is not a single instance of any company of Christians whose meetings were merely occasional, and who were not united for the purpose of stated fellowship as a church, in a particular place, observing the ordinance of the Lord's supper. And as we have no example, so we have no precepts for such things, not so much as a hint that they may be done. Should ministers, therefore, without the shadow of scriptural authority, consent to them?

4. As a precedent, the practice is dangerous; for if the scripture mode of observing the Lord's supper be departed from in one way, it may in another. If ministers depart from the regulations of the New Testament for the advantage of the sick, may they not be led on to do it in other cases, till even the purposes of faction shall be promoted by the practice?

It is not enough to justify it, to say that it is a

great loss to the individual who is deprived of the possibility of attending public worship, and therefore it is an act of Christian love to make up, in this way, the privation. We must not, in any instance, exercise charity at the expense of principle. The regulations of the word of God are not to be violated, even for the pious consolation of his people. Every one who is visited by an affliction which confines him to his house, is released from all obligation to observe this command of Christ, " Do this in remembrance of me." The duty to him is impossible, at least in the scriptural mode of it, and impossibility always supersedes obligation. If it ceases to be his duty, it ought no longer to be considered a privilege. All he has to do, is to submit to the privation, and not attempt to supply it in a manner unauthorized by the Word of God.

On the Causes of those Schisms which sometimes distract and disturb the Churches.

The existence of this evil, truth will not allow us to *deny*, nor ingenuity enable us to *conceal*.

Divisions in our churches produce incalculable mischief, since they not only prevent the *growth* of religion in the distracted societies, but they impair and destroy it; they excite a prejudice, a fearful and destructive prejudice, against the principles of independent churches, and extend their mischief still farther, by obscuring the glory of religion itself. Infidels, like vultures drawn by the scent of battle, hover over the scenes of these lamentable conflicts, ever ready to gorge their sanguinary appetite with the blood of the slain.

In searching for the *causes* of these divisions, we

are not to suppose, for a moment, that they are inseparably connected with the congregational form of church government.   Even if it were attempted to be proved, that these principles give more opportunity than some others, for the developement of the imperfection yet remaining in the Christian character ; yet as long as it can be shown, that they are fairly deducible from scripture, we are not to reject them, but only double our vigilance against the depravity of our own nature.   Even these evils are less than others which are connected with the systems of national establishments.   That uniformity which is produced by legislative enactments, is far more fatal to the interests of piety, than the occasional disturbances of those churches which are formed upon the ground of voluntary consent.   The occasional storm is less mischievous in its effects, than the stagnant and quiescent atmosphere which is purified by no breeze, and settles in the form of fever and pestilence on the face of the earth.   But what are the CAUSES of these schisms ?

I. Some of these lie with ministers.

1. A *defective education* not unfrequently prepares a minister to be the cause of much uneasiness in a Christian church.

Deprived, by the circumstances of his birth, of the advantages of education and cultivated society, he enters upon his academic pursuits with little knowledge both of books and of the world.   When he has been a student but two or three years, some injudicious congregation, captivated by a few sermons, solicits him to become their pastor.   He accepts their invitation, and with little information, still less acquaintance with the habits of society, he enters upon the duties of his office.   He soon betrays his ignorance, incompetence, and want of all those qualifications, which fit a person for government in the church, and prepare him for esteem in the world. At length, by the meagreness of his preaching, and the want of prudence and respectability in his conduct, he disgusts his flock, and a conflict ensues. *Both* parties are to blame; *they* in tempting him so soon to leave his studies; and *he*, in acceding to their wishes. *They*, however, are mostly to be censured; and so far as their own comfort is concerned, are rightly punished for plucking that fruit which, had it been permitted to hang till it was ripe, would have done them much service. A longer term of education would not only have given him more information, but more knowledge of men and things, and more capacity to conduct himself with propriety. Knowledge is power, by increasing a man's weight of character and degree of influence.

The churches ought to be very cautious of tempting students to leave the schools of the prophets, before the term of education has been completed; and this term in the present age ought to be *lengthened* rather than diminished. This is an age of *activity*, more than of *study*, and therefore a young man should be well instructed at the academy, for he is sure to meet with many interruptions to self-improvement, when he becomes a pastor. An inefficient minister is the cause of many disturbances; and that inefficiency, where it does exist, is to be often traced up to a contracted term of education.

Much, very much pains should be bestowed by all our tutors, not only to form the scholar, the divine, the preacher, but also the *pastor*.

2. In some cases, the evil is to be traced to the want of ministerial *diligence*.

Some, instead of devoting their time and their energies to the pursuits of the study, spend one half of their weeks in running about the country to attend public meetings, and the other in gossipping either at their own house, or the houses of their friends. The natural consequence is, that their sermons are poverty itself, or mere repetition of the same sentiments, in the same words. The people become dissatisfied, perhaps remonstrate in a disrespectful way; the minister takes offence; forms a party of his own; and the consequence is, a divided, distracted church. I believe one half of our church quarrels originate in lazy, loitering ministers.

3. Others are IMPRUDENT.

They live beyond their income, plunge themselves in debt, and their people in disgrace; or they speak unadvisedly with their lips, and involve themselves in litigation, with either their own friends, or persons of other denominations ; or they hastily engage in paper wars with their neighbours ; or they marry persons unsuitable to their character, and offensive to their congregation, and thus lay the foundation of uneasiness and dislike; or they become involved in *politics*, or public business, and thus neglect the interests of the church; or they speak ill of some members to others, and thus raise a prejudice and party against them in the society; or they let down their dignity by becoming the gossipping companions of some of their congregation. In all these, and many other ways, do ministers often prepare the way for dissatisfaction or schism. Piety and prudence in the ministerial character would prevent many of the divisions of our churches.

4. Others are men of *bad temper* ; hasty, impetuous, and peculiarly susceptible of offence.

They are easily offended, and frequently where no intention really existed to wound their minds. They then show their resentment in a way very unpleasing to the people. Many hard speeches and disrespectful terms drop from their lips, which are by some mischief-makers conveyed to the individuals against whom they were uttered. A fire of contention is soon kindled, and the whole church is enveloped in the flames.

5. Others are *immoral*.

They commit sin, and yet, attaching to themselves a party, they introduce great disorder and confusion into the society.

It is a point in casuistry, which I do not take upon me to decide, how far a minister might go in sin, and yet, upon his repentance, be authorized to continue his office as a preacher and pastor. I am inclined, however, to think, that if his transgression has been very flagrant, no penitence, however deep, no reformation, however manifest, can justify him in continuing an office, one qualification of which is, that he who holds it should be " blameless," and another, that he should have " a good report of them that are without." Instances have occurred, in which men who have fallen into gross sin, have been restored to penitence, and with it to their accustomed labour and success; but whether these are sufficient to justify the practice admits of a doubt. It has been alleged, that Peter was not discharged from the apostleship because of his crime, which was a very great one. But it may be questioned if our Lord's conduct in this instance can be drawn out into a precedent for ours. This was an extraordinary case under his own direction. Moreover, if our Lord's conduct in retaining Peter after his fall, is a precedent for *our* retaining ministers who have committed " presumptuous sins," his conduct in employing Judas, whom he knew to be a bad man, may be quoted as authority for employing such as are wicked.

The wonder is, that any church should wish to retain a minister, whose conduct has been grossly immoral, whatever fruits of repentance he might bring forth. It appears to me, therefore, upon the whole, for the interests of true piety, that he who has grossly violated the principles of Christian morality, should think no more of the ministerial office. It is of infinite importance to the interests of religion, that the ministry be not blamed, but its honour maintained with singular care.

6. The tenacity with which some ministers retain their situation, when their labours are no longer acceptable to their people, is another cause of uneasiness.

When from any cause a minister's services are no longer desired by his people, or the bulk of them, it is manifestly his duty to give up his situation as soon as he can procure another. Any attempt to remain in opposition to their wishes, is certainly wrong, as the union is not only formed on the ground of mutual consent, but for the purpose of mutual edification. Extreme cases may occur, such as a wish on the part of the majority of the people to introduce heterodox sentiments, in which a minister ought to remain, in opposition to the decided opinion for him to retire. In this case, a division is desirable; the majority (if any) ought to retire, and the faithful preacher of the truth to remain firmly at his post.

Let all ministers consider how much the peace and prosperity of the churches depend on their diligence, prudence, temper, and piety. Let them tremble at the thought of introducing strife and division to any part of the kingdom of Christ.

II. Other causes of division are to be found amongst the people.

1. A very large proportion of our schisms arise at the time of *choosing a minister.* This has already received a distinct and separate consideration.

2. *A hasty choice of an unsuitable person* to fill the pastoral office, has frequently ended in great uneasiness.

The people have discovered their error, when its rectification was sure to cause much trouble to the society. Upon our system of church government, it is not easy to displace an unsuitable individual, and therefore great caution should be observed in choosing him. Few men will venture to remain in opposition to the wishes of a whole society; but how rarely does it happen that an individual has *no* party in his favour!

3. A peculiar and dishonourable *fickleness* of disposition on the part of the church, is in some instances the cause of division.

They soon grow tired of the man whom they chose at first with every demonstration of sincere and strong regard. They seldom approve a minister beyond a period of seven years, and are so uniform in the term of their satisfaction, as to make their neighbours look out for a change when that term is about to expire.

4. Uneasiness has often arisen between a minister and his people, by the unwillingness of the latter to raise *the necessary support for their pastor.*

They have seen him struggling with the cares of an increasing family, and marked the cloud of gloom, as it thickened and settled upon his brow;

16

they knew his wants, and yet, though able to double his salary, and dissipate every anxious thought,
they have refused to advance his stipend, and have
robbed him of his comfort, either to gratify their
avarice, or indulge their sensuality. *He* remon-
strates; *they* are offended; love departs, esteem is
diminished, confidence is destroyed; while ill will,
strife, and alienation, grow apace. How easily
might all this have been prevented. A few pounds
a year more, given by some individuals who could
not have missed the sum, would have spared the
peace of a faithful servant of Christ, and, what is of
still greater consequence, the harmony of a Christian church. Can those persons be disciples of Jesus, who would put a religious society in peril,
rather than make so small a sacrifice? Let not
the voice of avarice reply, "Can that man be a
minister of Christ, who would feel offended with
his church, for not increasing his salary?" But
what is a minister to do? Starve? or beg? or
steal? If he is already living in luxury, and ex-
pects more, he deserves to be denied. But I am
supposing a case, where, in the judgment of candour, he has not enough to support his family in
comfort.

5. *An improper method of expressing dissatisfaction with a minister's labours or conduct,* has often
led to trouble in a church.

I do not pretend to say, that a minister occupies
a seat too elevated for the voice of complaint to
reach him, or that he is entitled (like his Master) to
an entire exemption from all that interference which
would say unto him, "What doest thou?" There are
times when it might be proper to remind a minister of some duty neglected, some pastoral avoca-
tion overlooked. But if anonymous and insolent

letters are sent him; if young, impertinent, or dictatorial persons wait upon him; if, instead of the modest, respectful hint of some individual whose age and station give him a right to be heard, he is schooled in an objurgatory strain, by those who have nothing to recommend them but their impudence and officiousness, no wonder, considering that he is but an imperfect man, if he feel offended with the liberty, and almost command the intruders from his presence. The apostle has spread over the ministerial character the shield of his authority, to defend it from the rude attacks of those who would act the part of self-elected accusers. "Rebuke not an elder, but entreat him as a father." 1 Tim. v. 1.*

6. *The domineering spirit and conduct of some leading members,* has often been the source of very considerable uneasiness to our churches.

If amongst the first disciples of Christ, there existed a strife for pre-eminence, and even in the churches planted by the apostles, it is not to be wondered at, however much it is to be regretted, that there should be individuals in our days, who carry the spirit of the world into the church, manifest a love of power, and struggle with others for its possession. Their property, and perhaps their standing, give them influence, and this unhappily is employed in endeavouring to subjugate both the minister and the people. No scheme is supported unless it originates with them; while every plan of *theirs* is introduced, almost with the authority of a

---

* This text *undoubtedly* points out aged Christians; but elder is a title given to the gospel minister; and there is much propriety in remembering the respect due to station. Mr. James pleads for kindness and love.　　　　　　　*Ed.*

law. They expect to be consulted on the most
trivial occasions, and if in any thing opposed, become resentful, sullen, and distant.   Little by little,
they endeavour to gain a complete ascendency in
the society, and watch with peculiar jealousy every
individual who is likely to become a rival.   The
minister at length scarcely dare leave home for a
Sabbath without asking their leave, nor can the people form the least scheme of usefulness without
their permission.   When they are at any time resisted, they breathe out threats of giving up all interests in church affairs, at which the terrified and
servile society end their resistance, consolidate the
power of their tyrant, and rivet the fetters of slavery upon their own necks.   At length, however, a
rival power springs up; a family of growing reputation and influence refuse any longer to submit to
the thraldom; opposition to unlawful domination
commences, the church is divided into factions, the
minister becomes involved in the dispute, distraction follows, and division finishes the scene.   Lamentable state of things!   Would God it rarely
occurred.   Let the leading individuals of our
churches, the men of property, and the deacons,
consider what mischief may be occasioned by the
least assumption of undue influence.   Let them
watch against the lust of power: it is a passion
most guilty and most mischievous: it arises almost
imperceptibly from their situation, and its progress,
like that of sin in general, is slow, but certain.
Let them conduct themselves with humility, and
deliver their opinions with modesty, and remember
that every exertion of illegal authority is an invasion not only of the liberty of the church, but of
the prerogative of its Divine Head.   Let them consider themselves as persons, whose opinion is to

have no other influence than that which its own
wisdom gives it; and that the measure of this wisdom is to be estimated, not by them, but by their
brethren. Let them seek for that humility which
can bear to be opposed, and that gentleness of temper which can submit to contradiction. Let them
distinctly bear in recollection that the church of
God is a society, where all are equals, all are
brethren; where the government of terror, or interest, or property, is unknown, but where love and
humility are to prevail, and no other rule is to be
acknowledged but that of Jesus Christ.

7. *The relaxation of scriptural discipline* may be
mentioned as another source of evil.

Where the church is unscripturally lax in the admission of members, and, for the sake of enlarging its
bulk, admits improper materials, it is certainly multiplying the causes of schism and decay. If a wall is
built with unsound bricks and untempered mortar, it
may stand for a while, but cracks and dilapidations
must sooner or later be visible in its structure. Thus
if men of unsanctified dispositions be admitted to the
church, what can be expected from such individuals
in a time of conflicting opinion, but fuel for the
flame of contention? The danger is considerably increased, where the individuals, improperly admitted,
are persons of property. If the ordinary rules of admission are dispensed with for the sake of bringing
into fellowship the wealthy and the worldly; if a less
rigid examination of their personal religion take
place, it is little to be wondered at that mischief should
ultimately ensue. For the sake of its glittering exterior, many a church has taken a serpent to its bosom; or, to adopt a scriptural allusion, has welcomed
an Achan to the camp, for the sake of his Babylo-
nish vest and golden wedge. If a rich member be

an unsanctified man, he has a double power to mischief; and in the time of trouble, this will be felt to the bitter experience of the church. "Whence come wars and fightings among you? Come they not hence, even of your lusts that war in your members?" James iv. 1. Of course, then, if we are careless in the admission of members, and receive those who do not give satisfactory evidence of personal religion, we are multiplying the sources of contention within our societies. Civil wars are to be expected in that country, which extends without caution the rights of citizens to aliens and enemies. Wolves admitted in sheep's clothing will worry and scatter the flock. As, therefore, we would not prepare for division and distraction, let us act upon scriptural principles, in the admission of members.

8. *The existence and prevalence of an antinomian spirit* is a fruitful source of schism in our churches.

"As every age of the church is marked by its appropriate visitation of error, so little penetration is requisite to perceive that Antinomianism is the epidemic malady of the present, and that it is an evil of deadly malignity. It is qualified for mischief by the very properties which might seem to render it merely an object of contempt—its vulgarity of conception, its paucity of ideas, its determined hostility to taste, science, and letters. It includes within a compass which every head can contain, and every tongue can utter, a system which cancels every moral tie, consigns the whole human race to the extremes of presumption or despair; erects religion on the ruins of morality, and imparts to the dregs of stupidity all the powers of the most active poison." . . . . Robert Hall.

This ruinous spirit has already disorganized or convulsed so many churches, that it is high time the tocsin should be sounded against it, and all good citizens of Zion take the alarm. It must be confessed, however, that it does not *always originate amongst the people.* A perversion of divine truth so monstrous, so mischievous and absurd, would hardly have acquired such power and prevalence, if it had not received the sanction of ministerial authority. I speak not now of those ministers who are the avowed and consistent patrons of the system, but of men more reputable, and whose strain of preaching is in general more scriptural; men who abhor the tenets of Antinomianism, but who are ignorantly the abettors of them. When such ministers dwell only on the doctrinal parts of revealed truth, and state these in a phraseology capable of misconstruction; when their preaching is exclusively confined to a few topics, and to a stiff, systematic exhibition of them; when a wretched taste for spiritualizing and allegorizing pervades their pulpit discussions; when the facts and doctrines of the gospel are *abstractly stated*, without being made the grounds and motives of social duty and moral excellence; when terms obviously scriptural are avoided, in compliment to a system which reprobates without understanding them, and their sermons are encumbered and disfigured with the phraseology of a false experience; when believers are flattered and caressed into a high conceit of their peculiar excellence; then, whatever be the preacher's tenets or intentions, must Antinomianism be generated and cherished. Ofttimes has this elfish spirit risen up to be the tormentor of the father that begat him; but if quiet till *his* head was beneath the clods of the valley, he has possessed and convulsed the church during the time of his successor.

To cure this evil, then, *let ministers be cautious how they preach.* Let them give a full exhibition of the doctrines of grace ; but at the same time let them exhibit these doctrines in a scriptural manner, as the basis of holiness and moral excellence ; let them introduce, in their preaching, all the varieties of revealed truth ; let them avoid the trammels of system, nor ever attempt to corrupt the testimonies of scripture by making a text say what it was never intended to affirm. The chief source of Antinomianism is in the pulpit, and let the first effort, therefore, be employed on the fountain, to render this pure and salutary ; and the next be devoted to drain off these streams, which are corrupting the churches.

When an individual, or any individuals, are known to cavil at the sermons of the minister, and to be employed in exciting a prejudice against him, by insinuating that he does not preach the gospel, they should be reasoned and expostulated with, both by the minister and the more judicious members of his flock. Every mild and persuasive method should be adopted and employed either to convince or silence them. If they cannot be convinced, they should at least promise not to trouble the church, or attempt to sow the seeds of disaffection in the minds of the brethren.* If they consent,

---

* Few persons can have any idea of the trouble which Antinomianism has caused in many English churches. The plague is in a measure arrested, but yet there are men, who would call all reference to Christian duty and watchfulness "legality,'' and complain of a preacher as unsound, who should insist on the importance of daily obedience to the law of God. Mr. James' language may appear strong ; but he has been fully justified by the existence of the character whom he has denounced. *Ed.*

on these terms, to remain in communion, they should of course be retained; but if again detected in the act of disturbing the society, they should forthwith be put away, as the troublers of Israel. I have known instances, in which ministers of great eminence and influence have suffered such individuals to remain in communion for the sake of peace, and have trusted to their own authority to prevent the mischief from spreading. This, however, is chaining the fiend, not casting him out, and leaving him to burst his fetters, when the hand that held him in vassalage is paralysed by death, and permitting him to waste and devour the church, under the rule of a younger or inferior minister. An act of authority, scripturally and seasonably exerted, would thus have destroyed an evil, which, by a temporizing policy, is bequeathed to a successor, who can neither destroy nor control it.

9. After all that has been said upon *distinct* and *specific* causes of disturbance, it must be admitted that the grand source of ecclesiastical distraction is the *very feeble operation of Christian principles on the hearts of church members.* There is not that solemn recognition and powerful influence of these principles which there ought to be. The two virtues of LOVE and HUMILITY, if prevalent, would effectually preserve the peace of the church against the evils of intestine commotion. Without these, even the kingdom of Christ, no less than the kingdoms of this world, is sure to be convulsed with faction, and torn by schism. As long as Christians suffer the passions of *men* to agitate their minds and direct their conduct in the assembly of the *saints,* so long must we expect to see even that holy convention liable to the distractions of mere

17

worldly communities.   Pride is the polluted and
polluting fountain of faction.   It is pride that makes
men turbulent and contentious ; that renders them
imperious, dogmatical and overbearing ; that drives
them upon the inflexible determination to have their
own way, and that makes them regardless of the
opinions and feelings of others.   HUMILITY and
LOVE would keep all quiet and orderly.   There is
one single passage of scripture, which, if sacredly
observed, would forever shut out the divider of the
brethren.   " If there be, therefore, any consolation
in Christ, if any comfort of love, if any fellowship
of the spirit, if any bowels and mercies, fulfil ye
my joy, that ye be like minded, having the same
love, being of one accord, of one mind.   Let nothing be done through strife, or vain glory ; but in
lowliness of mind, let each esteem others better
than themselves.   Look not every man on his own
things, but every man also on the things of others.
Let this mind be in you, which also was in Christ
Jesus."*   The observance of this single injunction
would ever preserve our harmony, and make our
church meetings to be scenes where all the air
is love, and all the region peace.

   And where is our religion, if we do not obey this
apostolic command ?   We must come back to the
first principles of practical piety, and cultivate the
passive virtues of the Christian temper.   We must
remember that Christianity is being like Christ, and
that unless we partake of that love " which suffer-
eth long and is kind ; which envieth not, vaunteth

* This passage of Scripture should be printed in large letters,
and hung up in the full view of the congregation, every time
they meet as a Christian church, that it might be referred to as
the rule of their conduct and their spirit.

not itself, is not puffed up; which doth not behave
itself unseemly, seeketh not her own, is not easily provoked, thinketh no evil, rejoiceth not in iniquity, but rejoiceth in the truth; which believeth
all things, beareth all things, hopeth all things, endureth all things;" we are only "as sounding brass
or a tinkling cymbal." The necessity of the Christian temper as a personal possession, and its importance, as a relative blessing, has hitherto been but
feebly perceived, and reluctantly acknowledged.
Amidst the controversies which have been carried
on about the doctrines of revelation, the spirit
of religion has been too much lost sight of. And
what, after all, is the doctrine without the spirit, but the body without the soul? Strange indeed it is, that men, who by their own confession
are apostate, ruined, helpless sinners, should want
HUMILITY; and that they who believe themselves
to be saved from hell by unmerited mercy, should
be destitute of LOVE!

Never, until we are brought to a more implicit
submission to the authority of Christ, and to a more
distinct and practical recognition of the principles
of true religion, can we rationally expect to see
Zion a quiet and peaceable habitation. Heaven itself would be a region of storms if pride could enter, or love diminish, in those realms of perfect
peace. We must crucify that selfishness, which
fixes its exclusive observation on our own gratification, and cherish that expansive benevolence
which looks upon the good of others. We must
contend who shall be *lowest*, not who shall be highest. We must seek to please, and not merely to
be pleased. In these things must our efforts begin,
to suppress and prevent the division of our churches.

Let ministers inculcate this temper from the pulpit, and exhibit it in their conduct; let private Christians receive the instructions and copy the examples of their pastors. Let both remember that HUMILITY and LOVE are the necessary fruits of our doctrines, the highest beauty of our character, and the guardian angels of our churches.

A Pastor's Sketches 1 & 2
by Dr. Ichabod Spencer

"*A Pastor's Sketches* is a sobering and challenging reminder that the Holy Spirit is the true agent of conversion. This book is urgently needed today when so much of our evangelism is patterned after current marketing methods. It has deeply convicted me to always seek to be in tune with the Holy Spirit as I minister to others." **Jerry Bridges**

"Dr. Spencer's *Sketches*, reprinted after a lapse of many years, are a veritable treasury of pastoral wisdom. They will amply repay careful reading by pastors and serious Christians in our day." **Maurice Roberts**

"The Spencer extracts are superb and will be of great benefit when printed. This is very sobering but enlightening material. It is quite contrary to much of today's practice and all pastors need to read it." **Peter Jeffery**

"Spencer is a master at flushing sinners out of hiding and directing them to Jesus Christ for salvation through Spirit-worked, simple faith. The responses he makes to inquirers is, in the main, biblical, doctrinal, practical, and experiential. His perceptive counsel certainly has produced much fruit. *A Pastor's Sketches* is a compelling read for pastors and Christian workers; its pages contain the nuts and bolts of biblical evangelism." **Joel R. Beeke**

"The republication of Spencer's sketches gives a rare opportunity for contemporary pastors, who have few if any models of pastors who understand the 'work of evangelism.' These sketches show a doctrinal depth and an experiential savvy perfectly meshed in one who had the cure of souls as his passion." **Tom Nettles**

"Ichabod Spencer was gifted by God with a passion for the pastoral care of souls. Any pastor desiring to shepherd the sheep, or to see God's elect drawn to Christ, will find page after page of wise and sage counsel in this work. It is practical, pious, personal, and precious." **James White**

List Price for each volume **$12.95**
Purchase both from SGCB for **$22.00**

Solid Ground Christian Books
Call us toll free at **1-877-666-9469**
E-mail us at **sgcb@charter.net**
Visit us on the web at **solid-ground-books.com**

SGCB Classic Reprints

In addition to *The Church Member's Guide* which you hold in your hand, Solid Ground has been privileged to uncover dozens of "buried treasures" from the past. Some of them include:

The Poor Man's New Testament Commentary by Robert Hawker, which has been unavailable for more than one hundred years. Spurgeon said of this commentary set, *"There is always such a savor of the Lord Jesus Christ in Dr. Hawker that you cannot read him without profit."*

The Sunday School Teacher's Guide by John A. James, which was written near the time Sunday Schools were first founded by Robert Raikes. This should be read by every Christian teacher.

The Devotional Life of the Sunday School Teacher by J.R. Miller, is an absolute gem of a book. Hundreds of copies sold in the first few weeks it was available again. No one who cares about the souls of others should fail to read this Christ-centered volume.

Christ in Song: Hymns of Immanuel from all Ages compiled by Philip Schaff, which contains hundreds of the finest hymns drawn from over 1600 years of church history. While only containing the lyrics, this volume will lead all the true people of God to worship.

A Pastor's Sketches: 1 & 2 by Ichabod Spencer, which has drawn the praise of great Christian's all over the world. In these volumes we view true evangelism in the trenches as a 19th century pastor from Brooklyn, NY presses the claims of Christ on those who are dead in their trespasses and sins. Life-changing volumes!

The Pastor's Daughter by Louisa Payson Hopkins is the true story of the faithful, patient and loving ministry of Rev. Edward Payson to his oldest daughter. This is parental evangelism at its best, as a godly, legendary pastor leads his daughter to conversion over a ten year period of time. Every parent must read this book!

The Young Lady's Guide by Harvey Newcomb is a veritable manual of life and godliness for young ladies who care about their souls and eternity. The perfect birthday or graduation gift!

Call us Toll Free at **1-877-666-9469**
E-mail us at **sgcb@charter.net**
Visit our website at **http://solid-ground-books.com**

www.ingramcontent.com/pod-product-compliance
Lightning Source LLC
Chambersburg PA
CBHW020448100426
42813CB00026B/3005

* 9 7 8 1 9 3 2 4 7 4 0 3 9 *